German GCSE Vocabulary

Your Malvern Guide

Val Levick
Glenise Radford
Alasdair McKeane

CONTENTS

Please note the following points:

- * These verbs take sein in the perfect and pluperfect tenses
- (*) These verbs can take sein or haben in the perfect and pluperfect tenses
- *sep* These verbs have a *sep*arable prefix
- *insep* These verbs have a prefix which sometimes separates but is *insep*arable here
- † These verbs are broadly regular, but have variations in some tenses. For further information refer to our publication 'Essential German Verbs'
- *irreg* These verbs are *irreg*ular. In lists where an irregular verb occurs more than once, only the first one is marked *irreg*
- *s.o* This means someone
- *o.s* This means oneself

- *pl* indicates that the noun or adjective is given in its plural form
- *no pl* indicates that the noun does not have a plural form
- *wk* indicates that the noun is a weak noun
- ‡ indicates that the noun is an adjectival noun
- To save space the feminine version of a person or profession is often not given where it is formed by adding -in (nen) to the masculine noun
- For reasons of space compounds of nouns may be given like this:
  der (Schul)Tag (e).........(school)day
  This gives two possible nouns, der Tag and der Schultag, with plural forms Tage and Schultage. In the longer noun, there is a capital letter at the beginning only
- *coll* indicates that the word is colloquial or slang
- *inv* indicates that the adjective never changes
- Page references are made at the end of sections to help locate other words which might be useful to the topic

- In Essential Vocabulary, high frequency words are marked in bold and common verbs, adjectives, adverbs, prepositions, conjunctions, question words, numbers, dates and times are listed to reduce repetition.

ESSENTIAL VOCABULARY

Adjectives

High frequency adjectives

alle *pl* .... all
alt .... old
fertig .... ready, finished
groß .... big, great, tall
gut .... good
klein .... little, small, young
schön .... fine, handsome, nice

Important adjectives

cool .... cool, trendy
furchtbar .... terrible
intelligent .... intelligent
jung .... young
modern .... modern
nett .... nice, kind
neu .... new
normal .... normal
toll .... great; mad
wunderbar .... wonderful

angenehm .... pleasant
arm .... poor
ausgezeichnet .... excellent
besondere .... special
blöd .... stupid
faul .... lazy
freundlich .... friendly
großartig .... splendid, great
klar .... clear, obvious
müde .... tired
nötig .... necessary
prima *inv* .... great
ruhig .... calm, quiet
schlecht .... bad
schwer .... difficult; heavy
sympathisch .... nice
unangenehm .... unpleasant
wichtig .... important

Other adjectives

artig .... well-behaved
attraktiv .... attractive
beide .... both
beschäftigt .... busy
brav .... well-behaved
dreckig .... dirty
erfolgreich .... successful
enorm .... great, fabulous, huge
enttäuschend .... disappointing
entsetzlich .... terrible
fabelhaft .... fabulous
fantastisch .... fantastic, great
freiwillig .... voluntary
gewöhnlich .... usual, common
goldig .... splendid, cute
hässlich .... ugly
hoch .... high
klasse *inv* .... great, terrific
köstlich .... splendid; hilarious
kühl .... cool, fresh
lautlos .... silent
lauwarm .... lukewarm
lebhaft .... lively, keen
leicht .... easy, light
lustig .... amusing
mies .... rotten, ugly, lousy
nackt .... naked
riesengroß .... enormous
rund .... round
sauber .... clean
sanft .... soft, gentle
schmackhaft .... tasteful; attractive
schmutzig .... dirty
sparsam .... thrifty
spitze *inv* .... splendid
stumm .... silent, dumb
taub .... deaf
unartig .... naughty
zufrieden .... content

Colours

blau .... blue
bunt .... brightly coloured, colourful
braun .... brown
gelb .... yellow
golden .... golden
grau .... grey
grün .... green
lila *inv* .... lilac, mauve
orange *inv* .... orange
rosa *inv* .... pink
rot .... red
schwarz .... black
silbern .... silver
violett .... purple, violet
weiß .... white
hellblau .... light blue
dunkelblau .... dark blue

Adverbs

High frequency adverbs

auch .... also, as well, too
da .... there
dann .... then, next
dort .... there
fast .... almost, nearly
ganz .... quite, fairly, rather
jetzt .... now
links .... on the left
oft .... often
plötzlich .... suddenly
rechts .... on the right
schnell .... quickly, fast
schon .... already
sehr .... very
so .... thus, in this way
vielleicht .... perhaps, maybe
weit .... far
wieder .... again
ziemlich .... rather

Important adverbs

gern .... gladly
gut .... well
immer .... always
leider .... unfortunately
manchmal .... sometimes
natürlich .... of course
sofort .... at once
viel .... a lot
zu .... too
zusammen .... together

Adverbs of place

anderswo .... elsewhere
dort drüben, da drüben...... over there
hier .... here
oben .... upstairs
überall .... everywhere
unterwegs .... on the way
unten .... downstairs

Adverbs of manner

allein .... alone
anders .... differently
bestimmt .... definitely
fließend .... fluently
glücklicherweise .... fortunately
hoffentlich .... hopefully
normalerweise .... usually, normally
sicher(lich) .... certainly
sogar .... even
sorgfältig .... carefully
vorsichtig .... carefully
wirklich .... really
auf diese Weise .... in this way

Adverbs of time

anfangs, am Anfang...... at the beginning
bald .... soon
damals .... at that (distant) time
danach .... after that
diesmal .... this time
drittens .... thirdly

eben .... just
endlich .... finally
erst .... only (with time)
erstens .... firstly
früher .... in the past
gerade .... just
gleich .... immediately
heutzutage .... nowadays
je .... ever
kürzlich .... recently
nachher .... afterwards
nie, niemals .... never
noch (ein)mal .... one more time, again
nun .... now
schließlich .... finally
täglich .... daily
vorher .... previously
zuerst .... first, first of all
zuletzt .... at last, finally
zweitens .... secondly
im Moment .... at the moment, currently

Adverbs of degree

besonders .... especially
ebenso .... just as much
etwa .... about
extra *inv* .... specially, on purpose
genug .... enough
insgesamt .... altogether
kaum .... hardly, scarcely
meistens .... mostly
mindestens .... at least
nur .... only
selten .... rarely, seldom
total .... totally, completely
ungefähr .... about
völlig .... entirely
wahrscheinlich .... probably
wenig .... little, not much
wenigstens .... at least
zirka .... about, approx.

Other adverbs

außerdem .... besides
äußerst .... extremely
doch .... yet, however
bloß .... merely
eigentlich .... actually
höchstens .... at the very most
immer noch .... still
jedoch .... however
liebevoll .... lovingly
mühsam .... painstakingly
sonst .... otherwise
umsonst .... in vain, free of charge
vor allem .... above all, especially
zweifellos .... doubtless
im Großen und Ganzen .... on the whole

Negatives

nicht .... not
nichts .... nothing
gar nicht .... not at all
gar nichts .... nothing at all
nie .... never
niemand .... no-one
noch nicht .... not yet
noch nie .... not yet
überhaupt nicht .... not at all

Prefixes

un- .... un-
mit- .... with
mittel- .... medium
nach- .... after
über- .... over
vor- .... in front, previously
wieder- .... again
zurück- .... back
zusammen- .... together

Verbs

Modal verbs

dürfen *irreg*................to be allowed to
können *irreg*................to be able to, can
mögen *irreg*................to like (to)
müssen *irreg*................to have to, must
sollen *irreg*..................ought to, should
wollen *irreg*.................to want to

High frequency verbs

arbeiten †....................to work
hören............................to hear
kaufen..........................to buy
lernen...........................to learn
machen........................to do, make
spielen..........................to play
wohnen........................to live

beginnen *irreg*............to begin
bleiben* *irreg*.............to stay
essen *irreg*...................to eat
fahren* *irreg*..............to travel, go
geben *irreg*..................to give
gehen* *irreg*................to go
haben *irreg*..................to have
kommen* *irreg*...........to come
lesen *irreg*....................to read
nehmen *irreg*...............to take
sehen *irreg*...................to see
sein* *irreg*....................to be
sprechen *irreg*............to speak, talk
trinken *irreg*...............to drink
werden* *irreg*.............to become
wissen *irreg*.................to know (fact)

Very important verbs

brauchen.......................to need
dauern...........................to last
fragen............................to ask
hoffen...........................to hope
sagen.............................to say, tell
suchen...........................to look for

bestellen †.....................to order (food, etc)
besuchen †....................to visit
bezahlen †.....................to pay (for)
enden †.........................to end, finish
sich interessieren †.......to be interested
kosten †........................to cost

ankommen* *irreg sep*...to arrive
aufstehen* *irreg sep*.....to get up
bekommen *irreg*...........to get, receive
bringen *irreg*................to bring
finden *irreg*..................to find
heißen *irreg*..................to be called
laufen* *irreg*................to run
schreiben *irreg*.............to write
spazieren gehen* *irreg*.....to go for a walk
tragen *irreg*..................to wear, carry
sich waschen *irreg*.......to get washed

Important verbs

anschauen *sep*..............to look at
glauben.........................to believe
schauen.........................to look
zeigen............................to show

antworten †...................to reply, answer
öffnen †........................to open
verkaufen †...................to sell
versuchen †...................to try

anfangen *irreg sep*........to begin
denken *irreg*.................to think
kennen *irreg*.................to know (person)
schlafen *irreg*................to sleep
schließen *irreg*.............to close, shut
verbringen *irreg*...........to spend (time)
vergessen *irreg*............to forget

Useful verbs

aufhören *sep*................to stop, cease
bauen............................to build
blicken..........................to look
fassen...........................to understand; seize

gucken .... to watch, look
holen............................ to fetch
klettern .... to climb
klopfen .... to knock (on door)
kriegen.......................... to get
passen (+ Dat) .... to suit, fit
planen........................... to plan
reden †.......................... to talk (seriously)
stoppen .... to (come to a) stop
teilen............................. to share
weinen .... to weep, cry
zählen .... to count

begegnen* † (+ Dat)..... to meet, bump into
erklären † .... to explain
erscheinen* *irreg* .... to appear
erwarten †..................... to expect
erzählen † .... to tell (story)
gebrauchen † .... to use, make use of
küssen †........................ to kiss
passieren* †.................. to happen
senden † .... to send, transmit

anhalten *irreg sep*......... to stop
ansehen *irreg sep* .... to look at, watch
bitten *irreg* (um)........... to ask (for)
ertrinken* *irreg* .... to drown
fallen* *irreg* .... to fall
fressen* *irreg* .... to eat (like animal)
geschehen* *irreg*.......... to happen
halten *irreg*................... to hold, keep
rufen *irreg* .... to call
schweigen *irreg*............ to be silent, shut up
sitzen *irreg* .... to sit
stehen *irreg* .... to stand
tun *irreg* .... to do
vorhaben *irreg sep* .... to intend

Prepositions

Prepositions + Accusative

bis................................ as far as; until
durch .... through
entlang.......................... along
für .... for
gegen .... against
ohne............................. without
um .... at (clock times), around; about

Prepositions + Dative

aus .... out of
außer............................. except for
bei .... at, at the house of
gegenüber .... opposite
mit .... with
nach .... to, after (time)
seit .... since, for
von .... from, of
zu .... to, at

Prepositions + Dative or Accusative

an .... on, at
auf .... on, at, in, into
hinter .... behind
in .... in, inside
neben .... next to
über.............................. over, more than
unter .... under, among
vor .... in front of, before
zwischen .... between

Prepositions + Genitive

anstatt .... instead of
aufgrund .... because of
außerhalb .... outside (of)
innerhalb...................... within
statt .... instead of
trotz .... despite, in spite of
während .... during
wegen .... because of

Common shortened forms

am .... (an + dem)
ans .... (an + das)
aufs .... (auf + das)
im .... (in + dem)

ins ....(in + das)
vom ....(von + dem)
zum ....(zu + dem)
zur ....(zu + der)

Conjunctions

Co-ordinating conjunctions

und ....and
aber ....but
oder ....or
sondern ....but (rather)
denn ....for

Subordinating conjunctions

abgesehen davon, dass
.............................apart from the fact that
als ....when (once in past)
als ob ....as if
bevor.............................before
bis ....until
da ....as, since, because
damit.............................so that (purpose)
dass ....that
indem............................while
nachdem ....after
ob..................................whether, if
obgleich ....although
obwohl..........................although
seitdem ....since
sobald ....as soon as
sodass ....in such a way that
während ....while
weil...............................because
wenn.............................if, when, whenever
wie ....as, how

Connectives

also ....so, therefore
angenommen, dass … .given that …
ausgenommen...............except for
dagegen.........................on the other hand
daher ....therefore
darüberhinaus ....furthermore
das heißt........................that is to say, that is
dennoch ....yet
deshalb..........................therefore
deswegen ....therefore
entweder … oder ....either … or
nicht nur … sondern auch
................................not only … but also
sowohl … als auch ....both … and,
not only … but also
trotzdem........................nevertheless
übrigens ....by the way
weder … noch ....neither … nor

Questions

High frequency questions

Seit wann …? ....How long … (for)?
Wann?...........................When?
Warum? ....Why?
Was? ....What?
Was für …? ....What sort of …?
Welcher/Welche/Welches ..... Which?
Wer? ....Who?
Wie? ....How?
Wie bitte? ....What did you say?
Wie ist …?....................What is … like?
Wie lange?....................How long?
Wieso?..........................Why?
Wie viel? ....How much?
Wo? ....Where?

Useful questions

Woher? ....Where … from?
Wohin? ....Where … to?
Nicht wahr? ....Isn't it? etc

Important questions

Um wie viel Uhr? ....At what time?
Wie viel Uhr ist es? ......What's the time?
Wie spät ist es?............What's the time?
Wie schreibt man das?..How is it spelt?
Wie geht's?..................How are you?
Wie weit ist es? ....How far is it?

Kardinalzahlen / Cardinal Numbers

0	null	10	zehn
1	eins	11	elf
2	zwei	12	zwölf
3	drei	13	dreizehn
4	vier	14	vierzehn
5	fünf	15	fünfzehn
6	sechs	16	sechzehn *(no **s** in the middle)*
7	sieben	17	siebzehn *(no **en** in the middle)*
8	acht	18	achtzehn
9	neun	19	neunzehn

20	zwanzig
21	einundzwanzig *(no **s** in the middle)*
22	zweiundzwanzig, etc
30	dreißig *(note the spelling with **ß**)*
40	vierzig
50	fünfzig
60	sechzig *(no **s** in the middle)*
70	siebzig *(no **en** in the middle)*
80	achtzig
90	neunzig
100	hundert
101	hunderteins
102	hundertzwei
141	hunderteinundvierzig
200	zweihundert
999	neunhundertneunundneunzig
1000	tausend
1100	tausendeinhundert/elfhundert/eintausendeinhundert
2009	zweitausendneun
321 456	dreihunderteinundzwanzigtausendvierhundertsechsundfünfzig
1 000 000	eine Million (spaces every 3 digits, no commas)

Remember that:

1. Years are usually stated in hundreds.
   So 1996 = neunzehnhundertsechsundneunzig
   Note that 2010 = zweitausendzehn
2. Where there is any danger of confusion, *zwo* is used instead of *zwei.*
   It is often heard in public announcements, and on the telephone.
3. Longer numbers - such as telephone numbers after dialling codes - are often written and read in pairs. So 01684 / 57 74 33 is pronounced as:
   Null eins sechs acht vier, siebenundfünfzig vierundsiebzig dreiunddreißig.
4. Cardinal numbers can be used as nouns, particularly when discussing school grades.
   Example: Ich habe eine Eins in Mathe *I have a 1 in maths*

Ordinalzahlen / Ordinal numbers

der erste	first
der zweite	second
der dritte	third
der vierte	fourth
der fünfte	fifth
der sechste	sixth
der siebte	seventh
der achte	eighth
der neunte	ninth
der zehnte	tenth
der elfte	eleventh
der zwölfte	twelfth
der dreizehnte	thirteenth
der vierzehnte	fourteenth
der fünfzehnte	fifteenth
der sechzehnte	sixteenth
der siebzehnte	seventeenth
der achtzehnte	eighteenth
der neunzehnte	nineteenth
der zwanzigste	twentieth
der einundzwanzigste	twenty-first
der zweiundzwanzigste	twenty-second

Die Uhrzeiten / Clock Times

In German, as in English, you can tell the time using the everyday way or the 24-hour clock.

12-hour clock (the everyday way)

Es ist ein Uhr	1:00
Es ist fünf Uhr	5:00
Es ist fünf (Minuten) nach fünf	5:05
Es ist Viertel nach fünf	5:15
Es ist fünf vor halb sechs	5:25
Es ist halb sechs (*careful!*)	5:30
Es ist fünf nach halb sechs	5:35
Es ist Viertel vor sechs	5:45
Es ist fünf (Minuten) vor sechs	5:55
Es ist Mittag/Mitternacht	12:00
Es ist Viertel nach zwölf	12:15

24-hour clock

Es ist ein Uhr	01:00
Es ist fünf Uhr	05:00
Es ist siebzehn Uhr	17:00
Es ist siebzehn Uhr fünf	17:05
Es ist siebzehn Uhr fünfzehn	17:15
Es ist siebzehn Uhr dreißig	17:30
Es ist siebzehn Uhr fünfundvierzig	17:45
Es ist siebzehn Uhr fünfundfünfzig	17:55
Es ist zwölf Uhr	12:00
Es ist null Uhr eins	00:01

Tage	Days of the week
Montag	Monday
Dienstag	Tuesday
Mittwoch	Wednesday
Donnerstag	Thursday
Freitag	Friday
Samstag	Saturday
Sonnabend	Saturday (North Germany)
Sonntag	Sunday

All days and months are masculine.

am Montag — on Monday
im Februar — in February

Monate	Months
Januar	January
Februar	February
März	March
April	April
Mai	May
Juni	June
Juli	July
August	August
September	September
Oktober	October
November	November
Dezember	December

To avoid confusion, in spoken German *Juno* is often used for *Juni* and *Julei* for *Juli*.

Daten	**Dates**
Heute haben wir den ersten September	Today is September 1st
Heute haben wir den zweiten Januar	Today is January 2nd
Heute haben wir den siebten März	Today is March 7th
Heute haben wir den fünfundzwanzigsten Mai	Today is May 25th
Heute haben wir den dreißigsten April	Today is April 30th
Montag, den 2. Mai	Monday 2nd May
Ich habe am vierten Februar Geburtstag	My birthday is February 4th
Ich bin neunzehnhundertsechsundneunzig geboren	I was born in 1996

Remember that *'in'* is **not** used with years in German.

Wann? When?

gestern .... yesterday
heute .... today
morgen .... tomorrow

am Vormittag .... in the morning
am Nachmittag .... in the afternoon
am Abend .... in the evening
am Sonntag .... on Sunday
gestern Abend .... last night
morgen früh .... tomorrow morning

morgens .... in the mornings
mittags .... at midday
nachmittags .... in the afternoons
abends .... in the evenings
nachts .... at night
montags, usw .... on Mondays, etc
dienstags, usw .... every Tuesday, etc

jeden Tag .... every day
jeden Morgen .... every morning
jeden Abend .... every evening
jede Woche .... every week
jedes Jahr .... every year

letztes Jahr .... last year
voriges Jahr .... last year
letzte Woche .... last week
nächste Woche .... next week
nächstes Jahr .... next year
im letzten Jahrhundert . last century
vor einem Jahr .... a year ago
vorgestern .... the day before yesterday
übermorgen .... the day after tomorrow
in zwei Jahren .... in two years' time

Es dauert ... It lasts ...

eine Viertelstunde .... quarter of an hour
eine halbe Stunde .... half an hour
eine Stunde .... an hour
anderthalb Stunden ...... 1½ hours
zwei Stunden .... 2 hours
einen Tag .... a day
zwei Tage .... 2 days
eine Woche .... a week
zwei Wochen .... 2 weeks
einen Monat .... a month
zwei Monaten .... 2 months
ein Jahr .... a year
zwei Jahre .... 2 years

Die Jahreszeiten Seasons

der Frühling .... spring
der Sommer .... summer
der Herbst .... autumn
der Winter .... winter
im Winter, usw .... in winter, etc

Opinions

Ich mag (nicht) … ....I (don't) like …
Ich spiele gern … ....I like playing …
Ich spiele nicht gern .....I don't like playing
Ich mag lieber..............I prefer
Das gefällt mir (nicht)..I (don't) like
Ich hasse......................I hate
Ich kann … nicht leiden...I can't stand …
Was meinst du?...........What do you think?
Ich denke, dass … ....I think that …
Ich bin deiner Meinung....I agree with you
Ich bin (nicht) einverstanden...I (don't) agree
Du hast recht ....You are right
Du hast unrecht ....You are wrong
Das stimmt ....That's right
Ich glaube ja ....I think so
Ich weiß nicht..............I don't know
Ich weiß nicht, ob … ...I don't know if …
Man sagt, dass … ....They say that …
Ich glaube nicht ....I don't think so
Ich schwärme für … (+ Acc)...I am keen on …

Meiner Meinung nach..In my opinion
im Gegenteil................on the contrary

Justifications and Opinions

Positive views

Es ist einfach ....It's easy
Es ist interessant...........It's interesting
Es ist lecker ....It's delicious
Es ist lustig...................It's amusing
Es ist nützlich ....It's useful
Es ist wunderschön.......It's wonderful
Er ist sympathisch ....He's nice
Sie ist nett....................She's nice

Es amüsiert mich..........It amuses me
Es interessiert mich ......It interests me
Es lohnt sich ....It's worth it
Es macht mir Spaß ....I enjoy it
Es gelingt mir einfach ..I can do it easily
Es klappt (gut).............It works (well)

Negative views

Es ist ärgerlich .... It's annoying
Es ist ekelhaft .... It's disgusting
Es ist kompliziert......... It's complicated
Es ist langweilig .... It's boring
Es ist schrecklich .... It's awful
Es ist schwierig............ It's difficult
Es ist unglaublich .... It's unbelievable

Es ist Blödsinn............. It's nonsense
Es ist Quatsch .... It's nonsense
Es ist eine Zeitverschwendung
.... It's a waste of time
Es ist unmöglich .... It's impossible
Es ist unpraktisch......... It's impractical
Es ist zu kompliziert.... It's too complicated
Es ist zu kurz .... It's too short
Es ist zu lang................ It's too long
Es ist zu schwierig....... It's too difficult
Es ist zu teuer .... It's too expensive
Es ist zu weit .... It's too far away

Es ärgert mich............. It annoys me
Es geht mir auf die Nerven
.... It gets on my nerves
Es langweilt mich .... It bores me
Es macht mich müde ... It makes me tired
Es passt mir nicht .... It doesn't suit me
Rosa steht mir nicht..... Pink doesn't suit me
Ich habe die Nase voll . I'm fed up with it
Ich habe es satt............. I've had enough
Ich kann es nicht schaffen .. I can't manage it
Es lohnt sich nicht .... It's not worth it

Positive/negative views with conjunctions

Ich mag das, weil: I like that because:
es interessant ist........... it's interesting
es mich amüsiert.......... it amuses me
es Spaß macht............. it's fun

Ich mag das nicht, da: I don't like that, as:
es langweilig ist.......... it's boring
es zu kompliziert ist..... it's too complicated

Excuses

Entschuldigung! .... Sorry, excuse me
Es tut mir leid .... I am sorry
Schade! .... What a pity
Ich habe das nicht extra gemacht
.... I didn't do it on purpose
Ich habe kein Geld .... I haven't any money
Ich habe keine Zeit .... I haven't got time
Ich hatte es eilig .... I was in a hurry

Neutral comments

Bitte .... Don't mention it
Gern geschehen .... A pleasure
Nichts zu danken .... No problem
Es ist möglich .... It's possible
Es macht nichts .... That doesn't matter
Das ist mir egal .... I'm not bothered
Machen Sie sich keine Sorgen
.... Don't worry
Vergessen wir es .... Let's forget it
Ich habe keine Ahnung
.... I haven't the faintest idea
Mit Vergnügen .... with pleasure
Es kommt darauf an ..... That depends

Begrüßungen Greetings, etc

Guten Morgen! .... Good Morning
Guten Tag! .... Good Afternoon
Guten Abend! .... Good Evening
Gute Nacht! .... Goodnight
Hallo! .... Hi
Auf Wiedersehen! .... Goodbye
Tschüs(s)! .... Goodbye
Grüß dich! .... Hello
Grüß Gott! .... Hello
Servus! .... Hi; Goodbye
Bis bald! .... See you soon
Bis später! .... See you later
Bis morgen! .... See you tomorrow
Wie geht's? .... How are you?
(Es geht mir) Gut, danke
.... Very well, thank you
Mittelmäßig .... So-so
Darf ich Eva vorstellen?
.... May I introduce Eva?
Angenehm .... Pleased to meet you

Herzlich willkommen! ..... Welcome!
Herein! .... Come in
Nehmen Sie Platz! .... Sit down
Bitte .... Please
Danke .... (No) Thank you
Danke schön .... Thank you very much
Vielen Dank .... Thank you very much
Entschuldigen Sie! .... Excuse me
Verzeihung! .... Sorry!
Gute Besserung! .... Get well soon!
Bitte schön! .... No problem
gleichfalls .... I wish you the same

Sehr geehrter Herr Koss ... Dear Mr Koss
Sehr geehrte Frau Koss .... Dear Mrs Koss
Alles Gute! .... Best wishes
Hochachtungsvoll .... Yours faithfully
mit freundlichen Grüßen .. Yours sincerely
mit bestem Gruß .... Yours

kennenlernen *sep* .... to meet s.o.

Die Religion Religion

anglikanisch .... anglican
atheistisch .... atheist
christlich .... Christian
evangelisch .... Protestant
gläubig .... a believer, religious
hinduistisch .... Hindu
jüdisch .... Jewish
katholisch .... Catholic
muslimisch .... Muslim
sikhisch .... Sikh
ohne Konfession .... of no religion

Das Wetter Weather

das Satellitenbild (er)....satellite picture
die Vorhersage (n)........forecast
die Wetterlage (n).........weather conditions
der Wetterbericht (e) ....weather report

die Aufheiterung (en) ...sunny period
das Gewitter (-)............thunderstorm
die Höchsttemperatur (en) ....highest temperature
der (dichte) Nebel (-)....(thick) fog
der Regen......................rain
der Schauer (-).............shower
der Schnee ....snow
die Sonne (n) ....sun
der Sturm (Stürme).......storm
die Temperatur (en)......temperature
die Tiefsttemperatur (en).... lowest temperature
der Wind (e) ....wind
die Wolke (n) ....cloud

der Donner....................thunder
das Eis...........................ice
die Feuchtigkeit............humidity
der Grad........................degree
der Himmel...................sky
die Hitze ....heat
die Kälte ....cold
das Klima (s)................climate
das Meer (e).................sea
der Mond (e).................moon
der Niederschlag...........precipitation (rain or snow)
der Schatten ....shadow, shade
der Sonnenschein..........sunshine

der Blitz (e)...................flash of lightning
der Druck ....pressure
der Dunst ....mist, haze
das Glatteis ....black ice
der Hagel ....hail
der Hochdruck ....high pressure
der Luftdruck ....air pressure
der Regenbogen (-bögen) ..rainbow
die Sicht(weite) .... visibility
das Thermometer (-) .... thermometer
der Tiefdruck .... low pressure
die Verbesserung (en).. improvement

Wie ist das Wetter? What is the weather like?

Heute **Today**

Es ist 30 Grad .... It is 30° C
Es ist minus 3 Grad ..... It is -3° C
Es ist bedeckt............... It is overcast
Es ist dunkel .... It is dark
Es ist heiß .... It is hot
Es ist hell .... It is light, bright
Es ist kalt .... It is cold
Es ist neblig (nebelig).. It is foggy
Es ist niederschlagsfrei .....It is dry
Es ist schön .... It is fine
Es ist sonnig................. It is sunny
Es ist stürmisch............ It is stormy
Es ist wechselhaft .... It is changeable
Es ist windig .... It is windy
Es ist wolkig .... It is cloudy
Das Wetter ist schlecht .....The weather is bad

Es blitzt........................ It is lightning
Es donnert.................... It is thundering
Es friert .... It is freezing
Es hagelt .... It is hailing
Es regnet .... It is raining
Es schneit..................... It is snowing

Es gibt Frost................. There is frost
Es gibt Gewitter........... There are thunderstorms
Es gibt Nebel .... There is fog
Es gibt Schnee .... There is snow

Morgen **Tomorrow**
Es wird kalt .... It will be cold
Es wird schön .... It will be fine
Es wird sonnig .... It will be sunny
Es wird windig .... It will be windy

Es wird hageln .... It's going to hail
Es wird regnen .... It's going to rain

Es wird Schnee geben .. It will snow
Es wird Frost geben...... It will be frosty

Gestern **Yesterday**
Es war kalt .... It was cold
Es war schön .... It was fine
Es war sonnig .... It was sunny
Es war windig .... It was windy

Es hagelte .... It hailed
Es regnete .... It was raining

Es gab Frost .... It was frosty
Es gab Schnee .... It snowed

Wann? When?

ab und zu .... from time to time
gewöhnlich .... usually
häufig .... often
manchmal .... sometimes
morgen .... tomorrow
neulich .... recently
übermorgen .... the day after tomorrow

Adjektive **Adjectives**
bedeckt .... very cloudy
besser .... better
bewölkt .... cloudy
blau .... blue
diesig .... misty, hazy
feucht .... damp
gewaltig .... fierce (storm, etc)
heftig .... heavy (rain, etc)
heiß .... hot
heiter .... sunny, bright
herrlich .... gorgeous
mäßig .... moderate
mild .... mild
nass .... wet
niedrig .... low
regnerisch .... rainy
schattig .... shady
schwül .... heavy, sultry
sonnig .... sunny
stark .... heavy (rain)
stürmisch .... stormy
trocken .... dry
trüb .... dull
veränderlich .... variable
wolkenlos .... cloudless
wolkig .... cloudy

bersten* *irreg* .... to burst
donnern .... to thunder
frieren* *irreg* .... to freeze
regnen † .... to rain
scheinen *irreg* .... to shine
schneien .... to snow
verändern .... to change
vorhersagen *sep* .... to forecast
wehen .... to blow (wind)
kälter werden* *irreg* ..... to get colder

LIFESTYLE

HEALTH

Die Körperteile **Parts of the body**

der Arm (e) .... arm
das Auge (n) .... eye
das Bein (e) .... leg
der Finger (-) .... finger
der Fuß (Füße) .... foot
der Hals (Hälse) .... throat, neck
die Hand (Hände) .... hand
der Kopf (Köpfe) .... head
der Magen (-) .... stomach
das Ohr (en) .... ear
der Rücken (-) .... back
der Zahn (Zähne) .... tooth

das Gesicht (er) .... face
die Gesichtszüge *pl* ...... features
das Haar (e) .... hair
das Kinn (e) .... chin
die Lippe (n) .... lip
der Mund (Münder) ...... mouth
die Nase (n) .... nose
die Stirn (en) .... forehead
die Wange (n) .... cheek
die Zunge (n) .... tongue

der Bauch (Bäuche) ...... stomach, tummy
die Brust (Brüste) .... chest, breast, bust
der Daumen (-) .... thumb
der Ell(en)bogen (-) ...... elbow
der Fingernagel (-nägel) ... finger nail
das Fußgelenk (e) .... ankle
das Handgelenk (e) .... wrist
die Hüfte (n) .... hip
das Knie (-) .... knee
der Nacken (-) .... nape of neck
der Oberschenkel (-) ..... thigh
die Schulter (n) .... shoulder
die Taille (n) .... waist
der Zeh (en) .... toe

die Ader (n) .... vein
das Blut .... blood
das Gehirn (e) .... brain
die Haut (Häute) .... skin
das Herz (en) *wk* .... heart
der Knochen (-) .... bone
die Leber (n) .... liver
die Lunge (n) .... lung
der Muskel (-n) .... muscle
die Niere (n) .... kidney
die Stimme (n) .... voice

Was ist los? **What's the matter?**

allergisch (gegen + Acc) ... allergic (to)
asthmatisch .... asthmatic
erkältet .... suffering from a cold
gesund .... healthy
krank ill
ungesund .... in poor health
unwohl .... unwell
zuckerkrank .... diabetic

behindert .... disabled
geschwollen .... swollen
schwach .... weak
sicher .... safe, certain, sure
wirksam .... effective

sich den Arm brechen *irreg*
.... to break one's arm
schlucken .... to swallow
sich in den Finger schneiden *irreg*
.... to cut one's finger
sich verbrennen *irreg* ... to burn o.s
sich verletzen † .... to hurt o.s, be injured
sich das Fußgelenk verstauchen †
.... to sprain one's ankle

Krankheiten	**Health problems**
die Allergie	allergy
der Durchfall	diarrhoea
die Erkältung	cold
das Fieber	fever, high temperature
die Grippe	flu
der Husten	cough
die Kopfschmerzen *pl*	headache
der Schnupfen	cold
die Seekrankheit	sea-sickness
der Sonnenbrand	sunburn
der Sonnenstich	sunstroke
die Tage *pl*	period
die Blasen *pl*	blisters
der Heuschnupfen	hay fever
die Magenverstimmung	indigestion
das Symptom (e)	symptom
schmerzhaft	painful, sore
steif	stiff
verstopft	constipated
der Insektenstich (e)	insect sting, bite
die Biene (n)	bee
die Fliege (n)	fly
die Mücke (n)	mosquito
die Wespe (n)	wasp
sich besser fühlen	to feel better
sich krank/übel fühlen	to feel ill
sich wohl fühlen	to feel well
krank werden* *irreg*	to fall ill
Mir ist kalt	I'm cold
Mir ist warm	I'm hot
Mir ist schwindlig	I'm dizzy
Es tut weh	It hurts
eine Erkältung haben *irreg*	to have a cold
Fieber haben	to have a temperature
Halsschmerzen haben	to have a sore throat
Kopfschmerzen haben	to have a headache
Magenschmerzen haben	to have stomachache
Ohrenschmerzen haben	to have earache
Rückenschmerzen haben	to have backache
Zahnschmerzen haben	to have toothache

Beim Arzt	**At the doctor's**
Beim Zahnarzt	**At the dentist's**
die Behandlung (en)	treatment
die Gesundheit	health
die Klinik (en)	clinic
die Krankheit (en)	illness
das Medikament (e)	medicine
das Mittel	remedy
der Patient (en) *wk*	patient
die Praxis (Praxen)	surgery
das Problem (e)	problem
das Rezept (e)	prescription
die Sprechstunde (n)	surgery (times)
der Termin (e)	appointment
die AOK	health insurance
das Attest (e)	certificate
die Blutprobe (n)	blood test
der Gips	plaster (broken bones)
die Kosten *pl*	expenses, cost
die Krankenversicherungskarte (n)	EHIC
die Operation (en)	operation
die Plombe (n)	filling
das Röntgenbild (er)	X-ray
der Schmerz (en)	pain
die Spritze (n)	injection
die Therapie (n)	therapy
die Versicherung (en)	insurance
die Wunde (n)	wound

einen Termin ausmachen *sep*
.... to make an appointment
behandeln ....to treat
besuchen †....................to go and see
im Bett bleiben* *irreg* ..to stay in bed
einatmen † *sep*.............to breathe in
einnehmen *irreg sep*.....to take (medicine)
einspritzen † *sep*..........to inject (a drug)
husten † ....to cough
Fieber messen *irreg*......to take s.o's temperature
stechen *irreg*.................to sting

sich ausruhen *sep*..........to rest
beißen *irreg*..................to bite
beraten *irreg*.................to advise s.o
bluten †.........................to bleed
sich erbrechen *irreg*......to be sick, vomit
Angst haben *irreg*.........to be afraid
ins Krankenhaus kommen* *irreg*
................................to go into hospital
den Arzt kommen lassen *irreg*
................................to send for the doctor
niesen............................to sneeze
pflegen...........................to care for, look after
schwitzen......................to sweat
sich übergeben *irreg insep*
................................to be sick, vomit
verschreiben *irreg* ....to prescribe
zittern ....to shiver

In der Apotheke **At the chemist's**
die Antibiotika *pl*......... antibiotics
das Aspirin® .... aspirin®
die Damenbinde (n)..... sanitary towel
das Dragee (s) .... capsule
das Fieber .... temperature
das Hansaplast® .... plaster, elastoplast®
das Hustenbonbon (s)... throat sweet
der Hustensaft (-säfte) . cough mixture
der Löffel (-) .... spoonful
der Saft (Säfte)............ (liquid) medicine
die Salbe (n)................ cream, balm
die Tablette (n) .... tablet
der Tampon (s)............ tampon
der Verband (-bände)... dressing
das Zäpfchen (-) .... suppository

das Aftershave.............. after shave
die Creme .... cream
die Seife....................... soap
die Sonnencreme .... sun cream
das Tempo (s).............. tissue
das Tempotaschentuch®...tissue
die Tempotaschentücher® *pl*..... tissues
die Tube (n) .... tube
die Watte .... cotton wool
die Zahnpasta.............. toothpaste

HEALTHY/UNHEALTHY LIFESTYLES

Ein gesundes Leben **A healthy lifestyle**

die Biokost .... organic foods
die (gesunde) Ernährung .. (healthy) diet
das Fett .... fat
das Gemüse .... vegetables
das Molkereiprodukt (e) ... dairy product
die Nahrung................. food
das Obst .... fruit
die Vitamine *pl*............ vitamins

die Abstinenz .... abstinence
die Aerobik .... aerobics
die Fitness .... fitness
das Fitnessprogramm.... work-out
das Fitnesszentrum .... gym, fitness centre
die Gesundheit .... health
das Gewicht .... weight
die Hygiene .... hygiene
das Leben..................... life
der Schlaf .... sleep
der Vegetarier (-)......... vegetarian
das Yoga .... yoga

athletisch .... athletic
fit .... fit
gesund .... healthy
nötig .... essential, vital
physisch....................... physical
vegetarisch .... vegetarian
in Form .... fit

abnehmen *irreg sep*...... to lose weight
sich entspannen † .... to relax
genießen *irreg* .... to enjoy
Diät machen .... to go on a diet
respektieren † .... to respect
superfit sein* *irreg*....... to be very fit
sich trainieren †............ to train
sich trimmen................ to keep fit
vermeiden *irreg*........... to avoid
wiegen *irreg* .... to weigh

einer Versuchung erliegen *irreg*
.... to give in to temptation
einer Versuchung widerstehen *irreg*
.... to resist temptation

Das ungesunde Leben **Unhealthy lifestyle**

der Alkoholkonsum ...... alcohol consumption
die Drogen *pl*............... drugs
das Fast Food .... fast food
das Fett.......................... fat
der Fettgehalt .... fat content
süße Getränke .... sweet drinks
das Rauchen .... smoking
Süßes .... sweet things
die Süßigkeiten *pl*......... sweet things
die Zusatzstoffe *pl* .... food additives

Die Folgen **Consequences**

die Bulimie .... bulimia
das Herzproblem (e) ..... heart disease
die Magersucht .... anorexia
der Raucherhusten .... smoker's cough
der Schlaganfall (-anfälle) .... a stroke
das Übergewicht .... obesity
die Zuckerkrankheit...... diabetes

fettarm .... low fat
fettig .... fatty
genügend .... sufficient
sitzend .... sedentary
übergewichtig .... overweight
unfit .... unfit
ungesund...................... unhealthy
zu viel Koffein............. too much caffeine

For **opinions** see page 10

Lebensmittel kaufen **Buying food**

Bäckereiprodukte **Bakery products**

der Berliner (-) .... doughnut
das Brot......................... bread

das Brötchen (-) .... bread roll
das Graubrot .... brown bread
der Keks (e) .... biscuit
der Kuchen (-) .... cake
das Schwarzbrot .... black bread
die Teigwaren *pl* .... bakery items; pasta
die Torte (n) .... gateau, flan
das Vollkornbrot .... wholemeal bread

Lebensmittel **Groceries**
das Bonbon (s) .... sweet
die Butter .... butter
die Chips *pl* .... crisps
das Ei (er) .... egg
das Eis, das Speiseeis ... ice cream
die Flakes *pl* .... cornflakes
die Haferflocken *pl* .... rolled (porridge) oats
der Joghurt (s) .... yoghurt
der Käse .... cheese
das Müsli .... muesli
der Reis .... rice
die Suppe (n) .... soup
der Zucker .... sugar

der Essig .... vinegar
die Gewürze *pl* .... spices
der Honig .... honey
die Margarine .... margarine
die Marmelade (n) .... jam
das Mehl .... flour
die Nudeln *pl* .... pasta, noodles
das Öl .... oil
die Orangenmarmelade .... marmalade
der Pfeffer .... pepper (spice)
die Sahne .... cream
das Salz .... salt
der Senf .... mustard

Die Getränke **Drinks**
die Cola .... cola
der Fruchtsaft (-säfte) ... fruit juice
der Kaffee (Hag®) .... (decaf) coffee
die Limonade .... lemonade
die (Mager)Milch .... (skimmed) milk
die Schokolade .... chocolate
der Tee .... tea
die Vollmilch .... whole milk

der Alkohol .... alcohol
das Bier .... beer
der Sekt .... German champagne
der Wein .... wine

alkoholfrei .... alcohol free
alkoholisch .... alcoholic

Fleisch **Meat**
der Braten .... joint, roast meat
die Frikadelle (n) .... large meatball
das Hackfleisch .... mince
das Hähnchen .... chicken
das Kalbfleisch .... veal
das Kotelett (e) .... chop, cutlet
das Rindfleisch .... beef
der Schinken .... ham
das Schnitzel .... escalope
das Schweinefleisch ..... pork
die Soße (n) .... sauce, gravy
der Speck .... bacon
das Steak (s) .... steak
die Wurst (Würste) ...... sausage, salami

die Ente (n) .... duck
das Geflügel .... poultry
das Hammelfleisch .... mutton
das Lammfleisch .... lamb
der Truthahn (-hähne) .. turkey

Gemüse **Vegetables**
der Blumenkohl .... cauliflower
die (grüne) Bohne (n) .. (green) bean
die Erbsen *pl* .... peas
die Gurke (n) .... cucumber; gherkin
die Karotte (n) .... carrot
die Kartoffel (n) .... potato
der Kohl .... cabbage
der Kopfsalat .... lettuce
der Mais .... sweetcorn

der Pilz (e) .... mushroom
der Rosenkohl *no pl* ..... Brussels sprout(s)
der Rotkohl .... red cabbage
der Salat .... salad; lettuce
das Sauerkraut .... pickled cabbage
der Spargel .... asparagus
der Spinat .... spinach
die Tomate (n) .... tomato
die Zucchini *pl* .... courgettes
die Zwiebel (n) .... onion

die Aubergine (n) .... aubergine
die rote Beete (n) .... beetroot
der Brokkoli .... broccoli
der Champignon (s) ...... mushroom
der Knoblauch .... garlic
der Kohlrabi (s) .... kohlrabi
der Lauch (-) .... leek
der rote/grüne Paprika .. red/green pepper
der Porree (s) .... leek
das Radieschen (-) .... radish

Obst **Fruit**

der Apfel (Äpfel) .... apple
die Apfelsine (n) .... orange
die Banane (n) .... banana
die Erdbeere (n) .... strawberry
die Himbeere (n) .... raspberry
die Orange (n) .... orange
die (Wein)Traube (n) ... grape

die Ananas (-) .... pineapple
die Birne (n) .... pear
die Grapefruit (s) .... grapefruit
die Kirsche (n) .... cherry
die Pampelmuse (n) ..... grapefruit
der Pfirsich (e) .... peach
die Pflaume (n) .... plum
die Zitrone (n) .... lemon

die Aprikose (n) .... apricot
die Brombeere (n) .... blackberry
die Erdnuss (-nüsse) ..... peanut

die rote Johannisbeere (n) .. redcurrant
die schwarze Johannisbeere (n)
.... blackcurrant
die Kiwi (s) .... kiwi
die Mandarine (n) .... tangerine
die Melone (n) .... melon
die Nuss (Nüsse) .... nut
die Stachelbeere (n) ...... gooseberry

Fisch **Fish**

die Fischstäbchen *pl* ..... fish fingers
die Forelle (n) .... trout
der Hering (s) .... herring
der Kabeljau .... cod
der Karpfen (-) .... carp
die Meeresfrüchte *pl* ..... sea food
der (Räucher)Lachs ...... (smoked) salmon
der Schellfisch .... haddock
die Scholle (n) .... plaice
der Thunfisch (e) .... tuna

der Hummer (-) .... lobster
die Krabbe (n) .... shrimp, prawn
der Krebs (e) .... crab
die Muscheln *pl* .... mussels

Wie ist es? **What is it like?**

Bio- .... organic
hausgemacht .... home-made
lecker .... delicious
natürlich .... natural

bitter .... bitter
frisch .... fresh, not frozen
gewürzt .... spicy
pikant .... (hot and) spicy
reif .... ripe
rein .... pure
roh .... raw
salzig .... salty; savoury
sauer .... sour
scharf .... sharp; spicy
süß .... sweet
würzig .... spicy

Rezepte	**Recipes**
auf kleiner Flamme	on a low heat
bei mäßiger Hitze	in a moderate oven
gut durchgebraten	well-done (roast/fried)
gebraten	fried, roast
gebuttert	buttered
gegrillt	grilled, barbecued
gehackt	minced
gekocht	boiled
geräuchert	smoked
gerieben	grated
gewürzt	spicy
gut	thoroughly, well
paniert	in breadcrumbs

die Gewürze *pl*	spices
der Ingwer	ginger
der Kümmel	caraway
der Pfeffer	pepper (spice)
das Salz	salt
der Zimt	cinnamon
die Zutaten *pl*	ingredients

das Basilikum	basil
der Knoblauch	garlic
die Petersilie	parsley
der Rosmarin	rosemary
der Salbei	sage
der Schnittlauch	chives
der Thymian	thyme

backen *irreg*	to bake
braten *irreg*	to fry, roast
füllen	to fill, stuff
gießen *irreg*	to pour
kochen	to cook, boil
mischen	to mix
schälen	to peel
schlagen *irreg*	to beat
schneiden *irreg*	to cut
vorbereiten † *sep*	to prepare
abschmecken *sep*	to flavour
bräunen	to brown, fry gently
würzen †	to season
zerschneiden *irreg*	to cut up
zudecken *sep*	to cover

Man braucht ...	**You need ...**
einen Teelöffel (TL)	a teaspoon (tsp)
einen Esslöffel (EL)	a tablespoon (tbsp)
eine Prise	a pinch of

Maße und Gewichte	**Weights and measures**
die Büchse (n)	tin
die Dose (n)	tin, can
die Flasche (n)	bottle
das Glas	jar, pot, glass
der Karton (s)	(cardboard) box
die Packung (en)	packet
die Schachtel (n)	box
die Tube	tube
die Tüte (n)	bag (paper, plastic)

100 Gramm	100 grams of
das Gramm (g)	gram
das Kilo (kg)	kilo
der Liter (l)	litre
das Pfund	500 g, pound (lb)

ein bisschen	a little
ein Dutzend	dozen
einige	a few
ein paar	a few
die Scheibe (n)	slice
das Stück	piece; item
der Teil (e)	part, share
der Tropfen (-)	drop
die Hälfte (n)	half
das Viertel	quarter

RELATIONSHIPS WITH FRIENDS AND FAMILY

Freunde **Friends**

der Bekannte (n) ‡........friend
der Freund (e)...............friend, boyfriend
die Freundin (nen)........friend, girlfriend
der Junge (n) *wk*...........boy
der Kamerad (en) *wk*....friend, mate
die Kameradin (nen) ....friend, mate
das Kind (er)................child
die Leute *pl*.................people
das Mädchen (-)...........girl

die Dame (n) ....lady
das Ehepaar..................married couple
die Frau (en)................woman
der Herr (en) *wk*..........gentleman
der Mann (Männer)......man

ärgern ....to annoy
ausgehen* mit *irreg sep*... to go out with
gut auskommen* mit *irreg sep*
...............................to get on well with
aussuchen *sep*..............to choose
besuchen †...................to visit
gern haben *irreg*..........to like s.o
kennen *irreg*................to know (person)
kennenlernen *sep*.........to get to know
(gut) leiden können ......to get on (well) with
mögen *irreg*.................to like
Schluss machen mit......to dump s.o
verstehen *irreg*............to understand

Die Freundschaft **Friendship**

die Freude.....................joy
die Gelegenheit (en).....opportunity
die Hoffnung (en).........hope
die Liebe.......................love
die Lust........................desire, wish
der Nachbar (n) *wk*.......neighbour
die Nachbarin (nen)......neighbour
der Optimist (en) *wk*.....optimist
der Pessimist (en) *wk*....pessimist

Die Familie **Family**

der (Halb)Bruder (-brüder)... (half) brother
das Einzelkind (er)........only child
die Eltern *pl*.................parents
das Familienmitglied (er)...... family member
die (Ehe)Frau (en) ....wife
die Geschwister *pl*........brothers and sisters
der (Ehe)Mann (Männer)...... husband
die Mutter (Mütter) ......mother
die Mutti (s).................mum, mummy
die (Halb)Schwester (n) .... (half) sister
der Sohn (Söhne)..........son
die Tochter (Töchter) ...daughter
der Vater (Väter)...........father
der Vati (s)....................dad, daddy
der Verwandte (n) ‡......relative

das Baby (s) ....baby
der Cousin (s) ....male cousin
die Cousine (n) ....female cousin
die Großeltern *pl* ....grandparents
die Großmutter (-mütter).. grandmother
der Großvater (-väter)...grandfather
die Oma/Omi (s)...........granny
der Onkel (-) ....uncle
der Opa/Opi (s)............grandpa
der Partner (-) ....partner
die Partnerin (nen)........partner
die Stiefmutter (-mütter) ...... stepmother
der Stiefvater (-väter) ...stepfather
die Tante (n) ....aunt
der Verlobte (n) ‡ ....fiancé
die Verlobte (n) ‡ ....fiancée
die Zwillinge *pl* ....twins

der Enkel (-).................grandson
die Enkelin (nen) ....granddaughter
das Enkelkind (er).........grandchild
der Neffe (n) *wk*...........nephew
die Nichte (n)................niece
der Schwager (Schwäger)...... brother-in-law

die Schwägerin (nen)............ sister-in-law
die Schwiegermutter (-mütter)
.... mother-in-law
der Schwiegersohn (-söhne).. son-in-law
die Schwiegertochter (-töchter)
.... daughter-in-law
der Schwiegervater (-väter)... father-in-law
der Stiefsohn (-söhne) .... stepson
die Stieftochter (-töchter)...... stepdaughter
der Vetter (n) .... male cousin

Wie ist er/sie? **What is he/she like?**

Adoptiv-, adoptiert.......adopted
alt ....old, elderly, aged
älter..............................older, elder
Familien- ....of the family
geschieden ....divorced
getrennt........................separated
jünger...........................younger
ledig, unverheiratet.......single, unmarried
verheiratet....................married
verlobt ....engaged
verwitwet......................widowed

Alter **Age**

das Datum (Daten)........date
die Geburt (en) ....birth
der Geburtstag (e).........birthday
das Geburtsdatum ....date of birth
das Jahr (e)...................year
das Leben ....life
der Monat (e)................month
der Namenstag.............name day

männlich......................male
weiblich.......................female
minderjährig.................minor, under 18
volljährig ....adult, over 18

Das Aussehen **Appearance**

die Augen *pl*................eyes
der Bart (Bärte)............beard
die Brille (n)................pair of glasses
die Glatze (n).............. bald patch
die Haare *pl* .... hair
die Kontaktlinsen *pl* .... contact lenses
der Oberlippenbart....... moustache
der Pony (s)................. fringe
der Schnurrbart .... moustache

blass .... pale
dick .... fat
dünn .... thin
groß............................. tall
gutaussehend............... good-looking
hässlich .... ugly
hübsch......................... pretty
klein .... short, small
mittelgroß .... of average height
schlank........................ slim
stark .... strong
untersetzt .... stocky
vollschlank.................. chubby, rotund

blond .... blonde
frisiert .... curly (frizzy)
gefärbt......................... dyed
glatt .... straight (hair)
kurz .... short (not long)
lang .... long
lockig .... curly (wavy)
rothaarig...................... red-haired
weiß .... white
mit Strähnchen............ streaked

blind............................ blind
schwerhörig .... hard of hearing
taub .... deaf

gehorchen (+ Dat)........ to obey
sich kümmern um .... to look after (person)
sich scheiden lassen *irreg*..... to get a divorce
sich Sorgen machen..... to be anxious
sich streiten *irreg*......... to argue
sich trennen *irreg*......... to separate
Kritik üben.................. to criticise

RELATIONSHIPS AND CHOICES

Die Leute **People**

der/die Alleinerziehende (n) ‡....single parent
der/die Alleinstehende (n) ‡ ....single person
der Ausländer (-) .... foreigner
der Erwachsene (n) ‡.... adult
der Fremde (n) ‡.......... foreigner, stranger
der Geschiedene (n) ‡... divorcee
der Jugendliche (n) ‡.... teenager, young person
der Junggeselle (n) *wk*.. bachelor

die junge Generation .... the younger generation
der Rentner (-)............. retired person
die Senioren *pl* .... senior citizens
die Witwe (n) .... widow
der Witwer (-).............. widower

die Beziehung (en) .... relationship
die Jugend .... youth
die Kindheit................. childhood

Der Charakter **Character**

die Art (en).................. manner
das Benehmen.............. behaviour
die Eigenschaft (en) ..... characteristic
das Gefühl (e) .... feeling
der Geist .... mind, spirit
die Gewohnheit (en)..... habit
das Glück .... happiness
der Humor .... humour
das Interesse (n)........... interest
die Laune (n) .... mood
die Persönlichkeit (en) ..... personality
der Unterschied (e)....... difference

Positive Eigenschaften **Positive Qualities**

der Charme .... charm
die Ehrlichkeit............. honesty
die Freundlichkeit .... kindness
die Freude (n)..............joy, happiness
das (gute) Gedächtnis ... (good) memory
die Großzügigkeit......... generosity
die Intelligenz...............intelligence
die Neugier ....curiosity
das Selbstbewusstsein...confidence
der Sinn für Humor.......sense of humour
der Stolz.......................pride
die Sympathie...............liking
die Vorsicht ....care, caution
die Vorstellungskraft....imagination

Fehler **Faults**

die Angeberei ....showing off
die Arroganz................arrogance
die Eifersucht ....jealousy
die Faulheit..................laziness
die Furcht ....fear
die Schuld (en) ....fault, guilt
die Selbstsucht.............selfishness
die Sorge (n)................care, worry, concern
die Wut ....anger

Positive Adjektive **Positive adjectives**

ehrlich..........................honest
geduldig ....patient
glücklich ....happy, pleased
guter Laune, gut gelaunt ... in a good mood
hilfsbereit.....................helpful
höflich ....polite
humorvoll ....humorous
komisch ....funny, amusing
optimistisch ....optimistic
ordentlich.....................neat, tidy
stolz ....proud

aktiv ....active
dynamisch....................dynamic
flexibel.........................flexible
fröhlich ....happy, cheerful
großzügig.....................generous
gütig.............................kindly
hilfreich ....helpful
klug..............................clever

offen ....open, frank
selbständig...................independent
unternehmungslustig ....enterprising
vernünftig ....sensible
witzig...........................witty

ausgeglichen ....balanced
begabt ....gifted
gut erzogen ....well brought-up
hoffnungsvoll ....hopeful
neugierig......................curious
schlau...........................clever, cunning, wily
selbstbewusst...............self-confident

Negative Eigenschaften **Negative Qualities**

angeberisch..................boastful
ängstlich ....nervous, shy
ärgerlich.......................annoyed; annoying
böse ....angry; naughty; nasty
doof *coll* ....stupid
dumm ....stupid
egoistisch.....................selfish
eingebildet...................big-headed
ekelhaft........................disgusting
frech.............................cheeky
schlecht gelaunt...........in a bad mood
gemein ....mean, nasty
humorlos......................humourless
launisch ....moody
schlechter Laune..........in a bad mood
nervös ....nervous
pessimistisch ....pessimistic
traurig ....sad
unangenehm ....unpleasant
ungeduldig...................impatient
unglücklich..................unhappy, unfortunate

deprimiert ....depressed
schlecht erzogen ....badly brought up
gehemmt......................self-conscious
schüchtern ....shy
seltsam.........................odd, strange

stur .... obstinate
unausstehlich .... unbearable
unbeholfen .... clumsy
verrückt........................ mad
verwöhnt..................... spoilt (child)

Neutrale Adjektive **Neutral adjectives**

ernst .... serious
erstaunt .... surprised, amazed
merkwürdig................. remarkable, odd

Engere Beziehungen **Closer relationships**

charmant .... charming
eifersüchtig .... jealous
empfindlich................. sensitive
enttäuscht.................... disappointed
ideal .... ideal
niedlich .... cute
reif .... mature
romantisch .... romantic
sensibel .... sensitive
treu .... faithful
verliebt (in + Acc) .... in love (with)

sich ärgern .... to get angry
ausgehen mit *irreg sep*...... to go out with
aussehen *irreg sep* .... to look, appear
sich benehmen *irreg* .... to behave
beschreiben *irreg* .... to describe
bewundern .... to admire
erkennen *irreg* .... to recognise
auf die Nerven fallen* . to annoy
auf den Wecker gehen* *coll* ....to annoy
gehören (+ Dat)........... to belong to
genieren † .... to embarrass
Angst haben *irreg* .... to be afraid
küssen † .... to kiss, hug
misstrauen †................ to mistrust
sich schämen............... to be ashamed
scheinen *irreg* .... to seem, appear
scherzen .... to joke
trauen .... to trust
übertreiben *irreg insep* .....to exaggerate

FUTURE PLANS (MARRIAGE AND PARTNERSHIP)

In der Zukunft **In the future**

die Absicht (en)............intention
die Ambition (en).........ambition
das Berufsleben ....professional life
das Berufsziel (e)..........career aim
die Laufbahn ....career
der Traum (Träume).....dream
das persönliche Ziel......personal goal

ein Studium abschließen *irreg sep*
................................to get a degree
freiwillig arbeiten †......to do voluntary work
in Kontakt bleiben* mit *irreg*
................................to keep in touch with
im Lotto gewinnen *irreg*
................................to win the lottery
ein Auto kaufen............to buy a car
kochen lernen...............to learn to cook
Führerschein machen ...to learn to drive
eine Wohnung mieten † ... to rent a flat
ein studienfreies Jahr nehmen *irreg*
................................to take a gap year
reisen............................to travel
die Welt sehen *irreg*.....to see the world
träumen ....to dream
Geld verdienen †..........to earn money
das Elternhaus verlassen *irreg*
................................to leave home
einen Beruf wählen ......to choose a career

Die Ehe **Marriage**

die Beziehung (en).......(personal) relationship
die Braut.......................bride
die Brautjungfer (n)......bridesmaid
der Bräutigam...............bridegroom
die arrangierte Ehe.......arranged marriage
der Ehering (e).............wedding ring
die Hochzeit (en)..........wedding
das Hochzeitsessen.......reception
der Kuss (Küsse)..........kiss
die kirchliche Trauung..... church wedding
die standesamtliche Trauung
................................civil ceremony
der Trauzeuge(n) *wk*.....best man, witness
die Trauzeugin (nen) ....witness
die Verlobung...............engagement
die gleichgeschlechtliche Partnerschaft
................................civil partnership

lieb haben *irreg* ....to like, love
heiraten †......................to marry
lieben ....to love
jemanden glücklich machen
................................to make s.o happy
unterschreiben *irreg insep*.. to sign
sich verlieben in (+ Acc)..to fall in love with
sich verloben † ....to get engaged
zusammenleben *sep*......to live together
zwingen *irreg* ....to oblige, force

Probleme **Problems**

der Alptraum (-träume) .....nightmare
das Alter........................old age
der Familiendruck.........family pressure
der Familienkreis..........family circle
die Lüge (n) ....lie (untruth)
das Missverständnis......misunderstanding
die Nachteile *pl* ....disadvantages
die Scheidung...............divorce
die Träne (n)................tear
die Trennung ....separation

getrennt.........................separated
verwitwet......................widowed

For **gap year** see page 83
For **working abroad** see page 90
For **jobs and professions** see page 86
For **education** see page 77
For **people and personality** see page 23
For **opinions** see page 10
For **celebrations** see page 76
For **religion** see page 11

SOCIAL ISSUES AND EQUALITY

Probleme **Problems**
die Beleidigung (en).....insult
das Internetmobbing.....cyberbullying
die Mode (n)................fashion
der Pickel (-)................spot, zit
die Popmusik...............pop music
das Schikanieren...........bullying
der Stress......................stress

Der Druck **Pressure**
der Elterndruck.............parental pressure
der Gruppendruck.........peer pressure
der Leistungsdruck.......pressure to succeed
der Mediendruck..........media pressure
der Notendruck.............exam pressure
der Schuldruck.............school pressure

die Arbeit.....................work
die Arbeitslosigkeit......unemployment
das Asyl........................asylum
die Ausbildung.............training
die Behinderung (en)....disability
der Benutzer................user
die Chancengleichheit..equal opportunities
die Diskriminierung.....discrimination
die Drogen *pl*...............drugs
der Geldmangel............lack of money
die Gesellschaft (en).....society
der Gesichtspunkt (e)...point of view
die Gewalttätigkeit.......violence
die Gleichheit...............equality
der Job (s)....................job (part-time)
der Mensch (en) *wk*......person
das Mobbing (s)...........mobbing
das Nachsitzen.............detention
der Nachteil (e)............disadvantage
der Rassismus..............racism
das Rauschgift.............drugs
die Schwierigkeit (en)..difficulty
die Sorge (n)................care, trouble
der Vandalismus..........vandalism

die Altersdiskriminierung...ageism
der Sexismus............... sexism
die Wirtschaftsflaute.... credit crunch

der Asylbewerber (-).... asylum seeker
der Außenseiter (-)....... the excluded
der Flüchtling (e)......... refugee

arbeitslos...................... unemployed
begabt.......................... gifted
benachteiligt............... disadvantaged
erstaunt........................ astonished
gelangweilt................. bored
schlecht informiert....... ill-informed
langweilig................... boring
mittellos...................... destitute
multikulturell.............. multicultural
Pflicht *inv*................... compulsory
priviligiert.................. privileged
rassistisch................... racist
schwach (in)................ no good (at)
süchtig......................... addicted
verärgert...................... angry, annoyed
verwöhnt..................... spoilt (child)
weit von der Stadt.....a long way from town

akzeptieren †............... to accept
ärgern.......................... to annoy
sich ärgern.................. to get angry
aufgeben *irreg sep*....... to give up
beleidigen †................ to insult
benachteiligen †.......... to disadvantage
diskriminieren †.......... to discriminate
einschließen *irreg sep*.. to include
sich erinnern an † (+ Acc)....to remember
erlauben †................... to allow
erröten* †.................... to blush
Spaß haben *irreg*......... to have fun
kritisieren †................. to criticise
sich langweilen........... to be bored

lügen *irreg*.................... to lie
fertig machen................ to humiliate
sich Sorgen machen ..... to worry
die Wahrheit sagen....... to tell the truth
unter Druck setzen .... to put pressure on
sniffen (slang) .... to glue-sniff
unter Druck stehen *irreg*
.... to be under pressure
sich streiten *irreg* .... to argue, fight
vernachlässigen † .... to neglect
verstehen *irreg* .... to understand
sich gut verstehen *irreg* mit (+ Dat)
.... to get on well with
verweisen *irreg* .... to expel

Wohlfahrtsprobleme Welfare problems

der Alkohol .... alcohol
die Droge (n)................ drug
das Heroin .... heroin (drug)
die Zigaretten *pl* .... cigarettes

Aids .... AIDS
der Alkoholismus .... alcoholism
die Betrunkenheit......... drunkenness (habitual)
die Bulimie.................. bulimia
das Komasaufen .... binge drinking
die Magersucht............. anorexia
die (ungeplante) Schwangerschaft
.... (unplanned) pregnancy
der Stress .... stress
die Sucht .... addiction (drug)
die Überdosis .... overdose

der Alkoholiker (-) .... alcoholic
der Drogensüchtige ‡ ... drug addict
die Entziehungskur ...... rehab
der Junkie (s)................ junkie
der Raucher (-) .... smoker
der Sniffer (-)............... glue sniffer

abhängig .... addicted
betrunken...................... drunk
drogenabhängig .... drug dependent
drogensüchtig .... drug dependent
magersüchtig .... anorexic
obdachlos...................... homeless
schwanger..................... pregnant
übergewichtig .... obese

angespannt.................... tense
bestürzt .... upset
gestresst .... stressed out
stressig.......................... stressful
zornig............................ furious, irate, angry

abnehmen *irreg sep* ...... to lose weight
Geld ausgeben *irreg sep* ... to spend money
Drogen nehmen *irreg* ... to take drugs
Drogen probieren †....... to try drugs
protestieren † .... to protest
rauchen .... to smoke
schaden † (+ Dat) .... to damage (health)
spucken......................... to spit
zunehmen *irreg sep* ...... to put on weight

Die Kriminialität Crime

die Aggression.............. aggression
die Brutalität................. brutality
der Diebstahl................. theft
der Drogenhandel .... drug trafficking
der Einbruch (brüche)... burglary
die Ermittlung (en) .... enquiry
der Fall (Fälle) .... case
das Gesetz (e)................ law
die Gewalt .... violence, force
der Mord (e).................. murder
das Rätsel (-) .... mystery, riddle
der Schrei (e) .... shout, scream
der Streit (e).................. fight, quarrel
der Überfall (Überfälle)..... robbery, mugging
der Vandalismus .... vandalism
das Verbrechen (-) .... crime
die Versuchung (en) ..... temptation

der Dieb (e).................thief
der Drogenhändler (-)...drug dealer
der Einbrecher (-) ....burglar
der Gefangene ‡...........prisoner
das Individuum ....individual
der Ladendieb (e)..........shoplifter
das Opfer (-)..................victim
der Polizist (en) *wk*.......policeman
der Richter (-) ....judge
der Rowdy (s) ....hooligan
der Staatsanwalt............examining magistrate
der Taschendieb (e) ......pickpocket
der Täter (-) ....criminal
der Zeuge (n) *wk*..........witness

das Gewehr (e).............gun
die Leiter (n)................ladder
die Waffe (n) ....weapon

der Beweis (e)..............proof
die Dummheit (en) ....stupid mistake
die Einzelheit (en) ....detail
die Entdeckung (en) .....discovery
die Erklärung (en) ....explanation
das Gefängnis (se) ....prison
die Geldstrafe (n)..........fine
das Motiv (e)................reason, motive
der Schaden (Schäden)..... damage
die Strafe (n)................punishment, sentence
der Streit (e).................argument
das Urteil (e) ....verdict
der Verdacht ....suspicion
die Wahrheit.................truth
die Zeugenaussage (n)..evidence

brutal ....brutal
gesetzwidrig ....illegal
grausam ....cruel
(il)legal ....(il)legal
kriminell ....criminal
mysteriös ....mysterious
schuldig ....guilty
unbekannt ....unknown

(un)gerecht.................. (un)just
unschuldig .... innocent
unzulässig .... inadmissible
wahr .... true
Er ist schuld .... It's his fault

anfallen *irreg sep*......... to attack
anzeigen *sep*................ to report to police
anzünden *sep* † .... to light (fire)
bedrohen † .... to threaten
begehen *irreg*.............. to commit
beleuchten †................ to light up
bemerken † .... to notice
beobachten †............... to observe
einbrechen* *irreg sep* .. to burgle
entkommen* *irreg* .... to escape
festnehmen *irreg sep* ... to arrest
fliehen* *irreg*.............. to flee
folgen* (+ Dat) .... to follow
lösen............................ to solve
sich nähern (+ Dat)...... to approach
stehlen *irreg*................ to steal
untersuchen *insep* .... to investigate
verhaften † .... to arrest
verschwinden* *irreg*.... to disappear

ahnen .... to suspect
bestrafen † .... to punish
einsperren *sep* .... to lock up
entdecken †................. to discover
erkennen *irreg* .... to identify
merken .... to note, notice
schlagen *irreg* .... to hit
stehen bleiben* *irreg*... to stand still
überraschen *insep* .... to surprise
verbieten *irreg* .... to forbid
verdächtigen † .... to suspect
vergeben *irreg* .... to forgive
verurteilen †................ to pass sentence
sich weigern................. to refuse
zittern.......................... to shake, shiver
zweifeln .... to doubt

LIFE IN GERMANY

Allgemeines **General**

duzen † .... to call s.o du
siezen † .... to call s.o Sie
die Heimat .... home area
gemütlich .... cosy, friendly

Bad + placename .... spa town
der Kurort (e) .... spa town
die Kuckucksuhr (en) ... cuckoo clock
der Trabi (s) .... East German car
der Weihnachtsmarkt ... Christmas market
das Hochdeutsch .... standard German
das Plattdeutsch .... dialect German
jodeln .... to yodel

Feiertage **Holidays**

der Fasching .... Carnival
das Schützenfest .... village fair
das Volksfest .... traditional festival

der erste Mai .... May 1st
der Maibaum .... May tree
die erste Kommunion ... first communion
die Konfirmation .... confirmation

das Oktoberfest .... beer festival
der Tag der deutschen Einheit
.... German Unification day (3 Oct)

Weihnachten .... Christmas
der Heiligabend .... Christmas Eve
der erste Weihnachtstag .... Christmas Day
der zweite Weihnachtstag ..... Boxing Day
der Tannenbaum .... Christmas tree
der Weihnachtsbaum .... Christmas tree
die Gans (Gänse) .... goose
der Silvester .... New Year's Eve
das Neujahr .... New Year's Day
Heilige Drei Könige ..... Twelfth Night

die Festspiele *pl* .... festival performance

Die Schule **School**

die Klassenfahrt .... class residential trip

sitzen bleiben* *irreg* ..... to stay down a year
versetzt werden* *irreg* .. to pass year at school

Essen und Trinken **Food and Drink**

das zweite Frühstück .... mid-morning snack
der Früchtetee (s) .... fruit tea
der Glühwein .... mulled wine
Kaffee trinken .... to drink coffee (in the afternoon)
Kaffee und Kuchen .... coffee and cake
die Konditorei (en) .... cake shop

Kleidung **Clothes**

die Bundhose (n) .... walking trousers
das Dirndl (-) .... ladies' traditional dress
die Lederhose (n) .... leather shorts
der Loden .... green woollen cloth
die Öljacke (n) .... yellow oilskin jacket
die Schiffermütze (n) .... dark blue sailor's cap
der Seppelhut (-hüte) .... green/grey felt hat

Sport und Spiele **Sport and Games**

die Bundesliga .... football league
die Formel-Eins .... Formula One
der Skat .... skat card game

Der Staat **The state**

der Beamte (n) *wk* .... civil servant
der Bürgermeister (-) .... mayor
die Gemeinde .... parish
der Landkreis .... district
der Wehrdienst .... military service
der Zivildienst .... community service

der Bundestag .... German federal parliament
der Landtag .... State parliament
das Bundesland .... state
die 16 Bundesländer ..... 16 states of Germany

LEISURE

FREE TIME AND THE MEDIA

Im Fernsehen **On TV**
die Dokumentarsendung (en) ... documentary
die Kindersendung ....children's programme
die Musiksendung ....music programme
das Programm (e)..........channel
die Sendung (en) ....programme
die Sportsendung..........sports programme

der Bericht (e)...............report
die Besprechung (en)....discussion
das Interview (s) ....interview
die Massenmedien *pl*....the mass media
die Nachrichten *pl* ....news
das Nachrichtenmagazin... news show
die Reklame (n)............advert
die Seifenoper (n).........soap opera
die Serie (n)..................series
die Tagesschau ....news
die Wettervorhersage (n).. weather forecast

die Krimiserie (n).........police series
die Quizsendung (en) ...quiz show
der Spielfilm (e) ....feature film
die Talkshow (s)...........talk show
das Theaterstück (e)......play
die Unterhaltungssendung
................................light entertainment

der Blu-ray®-Disk-Player (-)
................................Blu-ray® disc player
das Digitalfernsehen .....digital TV
der DVD-Spieler (-)......DVD player
die Fernbedienung........remote control
das Kabelfernsehen.......cable TV
der Podcast (s).............podcast
das Satellitenfernsehen ......satellite TV
die Satellitenschüssel (n)...satellite dish
der Ton (Töne) ....sound, audio
der Videorekorder (-)....video recorder

der Zuschauer (-).......... viewer

aktuell .... current
interviewen .... to interview
zappen.......................... to channel-hop

For **opinions** see page 10

Die Musik **Music**
das Album (Alben)....... album
der Jazz .... jazz
die Melodie................. tune
die klassische Musik.... classical music
die Popmusik .... pop music
der Rap......................... rap
der Rock....................... rock
die Volksmusik........... traditional music

aufgenommen .... recorded
live .... live (e.g. radio)

die CD (s) .... compact disc, CD
der CD-Spieler (-)........ CD player
der MP3-Player (-) .... MP3 player
die Stereoanlage (n)..... stereo system
der Walkman® (s) .... walkman®

die Blockflöte (n)......... recorder
die Geige (n)................ violin
die Gitarre (n) .... guitar
das Instrument (e) .... instrument
das Keyboard (s) .... keyboard
die Klarinette (n) .... clarinet
das Klavier (e).............. piano (upright)
die Posaune (n) .... trombone
die Querflöte (n) .... flute
das Schlagzeug............. drum kit
die Trompete (n).......... trumpet

die Art (en)..................type, sort
die Band (s).................group
der Chor (Chöre).........choir
der Hit (s)....................hit song (in English)
das Lied (er).................song
das Orchester (-)..........orchestra, band
der Schlager (-)............hit song (in German)
der Song (s).................song

im Chor singen *irreg*....to sing in the choir
Klavier spielen............to play the piano
Musik spielen..............to play music
Schlagzeug spielen.......to play the drums

laut...............................loudly
leise.............................quietly

anmachen *sep*..............to switch on
aufnehmen *irreg sep*....to record
ausmachen *sep*............to switch off
ausschalten † *sep*.........to switch off
einschalten † *sep*.........to switch on
Musik hören................to listen to music
lachen..........................to laugh
musizieren †.................to make music
schätzen........................to appreciate
üben.............................to practise
zuhören *sep*.................to listen (to)
zusehen *irreg sep*.........to watch

For **music** also see page 30

Computerspiele — **Computer games**

das Computerspiel (e)...computer game
der Joystick (s)............joystick
die Spielkonsole (n).....games console
das Videospiel (e).........video game

Im Kino — **At the cinema**

die Eintrittskarte (n).....ticket
der Film (e)..................film
die Figur (en)...............character
der Held (en) *wk*...........hero
die Heldin (nen)............heroine
die Person (en).............character
der Schurke (n) *wk*........villain

Was gibt es? — **What's on?**

der Abenteuerfilm (e)...adventure film
der Dokumentarfilm (e)....documentary film
der Gruselfilm (e).........horror film
der Horrorfilm (e).........horror film
die Komödie (n)...........comedy film
der Kriegsfilm (e).........war film
der Krimi (s).................detective film
der Kriminalfilm (e).....detective film
der Liebesfilm (e).........love film
der Science-Fiction-Film (e)
...............................science fiction film
der Spielfilm (e)...........feature film
der Spionagefilm (e).....spy film
der Thriller (s).............thriller
der Western (s)............Western
der Zeichentrickfilm (e).....cartoon

Lieblings- ....favourite
im Originalton ....original soundtrack
mit Untertiteln ....subtitled
synchronisiert ....dubbed
auf Deutsch..................in German
Es handelt sich um … .It is about …

Das Theater — **The theatre**

die Aufführung (en)......production
das Ballett (e)................ballet
die Bühne (n)................stage (drama)
das Drama (Dramen).....drama
die Handlung (en).........plot
die Komödie (n)...........comedy
die Nachmittagsvorstellung (en)
...............................matinée
die Oper (n).................opera
die Pause (n)................interval
das Publikum ....audience
die Rolle (n).................role

das Schauspiel (e) .... play
das Theaterstück (e)...... play
die Tragödie (n)........... tragedy
die Truppe (n)............... theatre company
die Vorstellung (en)...... performance

die Garderobe (n) .... cloakroom
im Parkett .... in the stalls
im ersten Rang............. in the circle

aufführen *sep* .... to produce

Eintrittskarten kaufen **Buying tickets**
der Eintritt (e) .... entrance (price)
die Eintrittskarte (n) ..... ticket
der Eintrittspreis (e)...... entrance price
die Ermäßigung (en)..... reduction
der Platz (Plätze) .... seat
der Preis (e) .... cost, price
die Schülerermäßigung .... school student rate
der Sitz (e) .... seat

ermäßigt........................ at a reduced rate
im Voraus .... in advance
zusätzlich...................... additional, further

der Erwachsene (n) ‡.... adult
die Gruppe (n) .... group
das Kind (er) .... child
der Schüler (-)............... school student
die Schülerin (nen) .... school student
der Student (en) *wk*....... university student
die Studentin (nen) .... university student

Wann ist es? **When is it?**
täglich........................... daily
am Wochenende .... at the weekend
jede Woche................... every week
wöchentlich .... weekly
monatlich...................... monthly
jährlich.......................... annually

Wie ist es? **What is it like?**
aufregend .... exciting
außergewöhnlich.......... extraordinary
echt gut .... super
eindrucksvoll .... impressive
einmalig....................... superb; unique
hervorragend............... excellent
lächerlich .... ridiculous
langweilig .... boring
nutzlos .... useless
schlimm .... bad
schrecklich.................. awful
seltsam .... funny (odd)
sensationell .... sensational
spannend...................... exciting
super .... very good, super
tragisch .... tragic
unangenehm................ unpleasant
widerlich...................... revolting

Wo treffen wir uns? **Where shall we meet?**
am Bahnhof .... at the station
an der Bushaltestelle.... at the bus stop
im Café .... in the café
in der Eisdiele............. in the ice cream bar
im Internet-Café.......... in the internet café
vor dem Kino.............. outside the cinema
in der Pizzeria............. in the pizzeria
im Restaurant............... in the restaurant
wie verabredet .... as arranged

begleiten † .... to go with
beschließen *irreg* .... to decide
besuchen † .... to visit
einladen *irreg sep* .... to invite
entscheiden *irreg* .... to decide
sich entschuldigen † .... to be sorry
stattfinden *irreg sep*..... to take place
treffen *irreg* .... to meet
sich verabreden †......... to arrange to meet
vorschlagen *irreg sep* .. to suggest
warten auf † (+ Acc).... to wait for

Prominenten **Celebrities**

die Band (s) .... group, band
der Fußballer (-) .... footballer
die Gruppe (n) .... group
der Komödiant (en) *wk*..... comedian
die Komödiantin (nen)..... comedian
der Künstler (-)............ artist
das Mitglied (er) .... member
der Moderator (en) .... presenter
der Sänger (-)............... singer
die Sängerin (nen) .... singer
der Schauspieler (-) ...... actor
die Schauspielerin (nen)... actor
der Schriftsteller (-) ...... writer
der Star (s) .... filmstar

der Artikel (-) .... article
das Bild (er) .... image, picture
der Fernsehstar (s) .... TV personality
die Paparazzi *pl* .... paparazzi
die Tournee (s) .... tour (eg musician)

bekannt .... well-known
berühmt .... famous
komisch .... funny, amusing
sensationell................... sensational

im Fernsehen erscheinen* *irreg*
.... to appear on TV
über Klatsch und Tratsch Bescheid wissen
.... to know all the gossip

Die Werbung **Advertising**

das Fernsehen .... television
die Illustrierte (n) ‡ ...... magazine
das Internet .... internet
der Katalog (e)............. catalogue
die Litfaßsäule (n) .... advertising pillar
das Magazin (e) .... magazine
die Marke (n)............... brand
Marken- .... high quality
die Markentreue .... brand loyalty
das Marketing .... marketing
die Meinungsumfrage (n). opinion poll
das Plakat (e) ....poster
das Poster (-)................poster
das Radio ....radio
die Reklame (n)...........advert, advertising
der Rundfunk................radio
der Werbespot (s) ....advertising slot
der Werbespruch (-sprüche)
.... advertising slogan
die Zeitschrift (en)........magazine
die Zeitung (en)...........newspaper

Die Kleinanzeigen **Small ads**

die Anzeige (n).............advert
die Belohnung ....reward
die Ferienwohnung (en) ... holiday home
das Haus (Häuser).........house
die Hochzeit (en)..........marriage, wedding
das Mountainbike (s) ....mountain bike
das Produkt (e).............products
das Rad (Räder) ....bike
das Sonderangebot (e)...special offer
der Urlaub.....................holidays
das Vergnügen ....pleasure
der Verkauf (-käufe) .....sale
der Wagen (-)................car
der Wert (e) ....value
die Wohnung (en).........flat

billiger ....cheaper
geeignet ....appropriate, suitable
preiswert.......................cheap, good value
wertvoll ....valuable

im Angebot...................on offer
als Anzahlung...............as a deposit
aus zweiter Hand ....second-hand
niedrige Preise *pl*..........low prices
mit Rabatt ....at a discount
im Schlussverkauf ....in the sales
zu verkaufen ....for sale
zu vermieten ....for hire
zu verschenken ....to give away for free

FREE TIME ACTIVITIES

Der Sport **Sport**

die Atmosphäre ....atmosphere
die Ferien *pl* ....holidays
die Freizeit....................free time
das Hobby (s)................hobby
die Möglichkeit (en).....possibility, facility
die Sportart (en) ....(type of) sport
die Unterhaltung...........entertainment
das Wochenende (n) .....weekend

der Amateur (e) ....amateur
der Fan (s)......................fan, supporter
die Mannschaft (en)......team
der Meister (-)...............champion
das Mitglied (er) ....member
der Profi (s)...................professional
der Spieler (-) ....player

die Eishalle (n) ....skating rink
das Freizeitzentrum .....leisure centre
der Fußballverein (e) ....football club
der Platz (Plätze) ....pitch, court
die Reitschule (n) ....riding school
der Sportplatz (-plätze)......sports ground
das Sportzentrum (-zentren) .. sports centre
das Stadion (Stadien)....stadium
der Tennisclub (s).........tennis club
der Verein (e)................club

das Endspiel (e) ....final
die Gebühr (en) ....fee
die Liga (Ligen)............league
die Meisterschaft (en)...championship
der Pokal (e) ....cup, trophy
das Spiel (e) ....match, game
das Tor (e).....................goal
das Turnier (e) ....tournament
der Wettbewerb (e).......competition, contest

Welchen Sport treibst du gern?
Which sport do you like?

das Angeln .... fishing
das Badminton .... badminton
der Basketball .... basketball
der Fußball................... football
das Golf......................... golf
die Gymnastik.............. gymnastics
das Hockey................... hockey
das Jogging .... jogging
das Kricket................... cricket
die Leichtathletik......... athletics
der Netball, Korbball ... netball
das Radfahren .... cycling
das Reiten..................... horse riding
das Rugby..................... rugby
das Schwimmen .... swimming
das Tennis .... tennis
das Tischtennis............. table tennis
der Volleyball .... volleyball

das Bergsteigen .... mountaineering
der Boxsport .... boxing
das Darts .... darts
das Drachenfliegen....... hang gliding
der Handball .... handball
der Hochsprung............ high jump
das Judo .... judo
die Kampfsportarten *pl*......martial arts
das Kegeln.................... bowling
das Rollschuhlaufen..... roller skating
das Schlittschuhlaufen ......ice skating
das Segeln .... sailing
das Skilaufen................ skiing
das Tanzen .... dancing
der Wassersport .... water sports
der Weitsprung .... long jump
das Windsurfen .... wind surfing
der Wintersport............ winter sports

Das Spiel **The match**
der Anfang.................... start, beginning
der Beginn .... start, beginning
der Einwurf (-würfe) .... throw-in
die Niederlage (n) .... defeat
der Sieg (e) .... win
das Tor (e) .... goal

viele Leute.................... lots of people
die Mannschaft (en) ..... team
der Schiedsrichter (-).... referee
der Spieler (-) .... player
der Torwart (e) .... goalkeeper
der Zuschauer (-) .... spectator
die Zuschauer *pl*........... crowd

ehrenamtlich................. as a volunteer
rechts außen .... outside right

gewinnen *irreg* .... to win
Glück haben *irreg* .... to be lucky
ein Tor schießen *irreg*.. to score a goal
schlagen *irreg*............... to beat
teilnehmen an (+ Dat) *irreg sep*
.... to take part in
unentschieden spielen .. to draw
unterstützen † *insep* ..... to support
verlieren *irreg* .... to lose
verteidigen †................. to defend

For **sport** see page 34

Die Sportausrüstung **Sports equipment**
der Badeanzug (-züge) . swimsuit
der Ball (Bälle)............. ball
der Fußball (-bälle)....... football
die Fußballschuhe *pl* .... football boots
der Helm (e) .... helmet
der Hockeyschläger (-)..... hockey stick
die Inliner *pl* .... inline skates
der Kricketschläger (-) ..... cricket bat
das Mountainbike (s).... mountain bike
die Rollschuhe *pl* .... roller skates
der Ski (s) .... ski
das Surfbrett (er)........... surfboard
der Tennisschläger (-)... tennis racket
die Sportschuhe *pl*........ trainers (shoes)
die Turnschuhe *pl*......... trainers (shoes)

Wie ist es? **What is it like?**
amüsant .... funny
andere .... other
anstrengend.................. tiring
astrein *coll* .... great, super
aufregend .... exciting
beliebt .... popular
echt .... real, genuine
echt gut .... really good
eindrucksvoll .... impressive
einmalig .... great, brilliant
energisch....................... energetic
ermüdend .... tiring
fair .... fair
nicht gestattet............... not allowed
nutzlos .... useless
nicht schlecht............... not bad
schrecklich.................... awful
sportlich........................ sporty, keen on sport
super .... super
unfair .... unfair

Was machst du? **What do you do?**
fit bleiben* *irreg* .... to keep fit
spazieren gehen* *irreg* ..... to go for a walk
schwimmen (*) *irreg*.... to swim
Fußball spielen .... to play football
Sport treiben *irreg* .... to do sport
wandern* .... to hike, go for a long walk

Rad fahren* *irreg* .... to cycle
Rollschuh fahren* .... to roller-skate
Skateboard fahren*....... to skateboard
Ski fahren* .... to ski
Schlittschuh laufen* *irreg* .. to skate
Ski laufen* .... to ski
eine Radtour machen.... to go for a bike ride

angeln gehen* *irreg*......to go fishing
sich anmelden † *sep* .....to enrol
ausrüsten † *sep* ....to equip
fangen *irreg*..................to catch (fish)
joggen ....to jog
reiten* *irreg*..................to go horse riding
segeln............................to go sailing
springen* *irreg*.............to jump, leap
teilnehmen *irreg sep*.....to participate
werfen *irreg*..................to throw
windsurfen.....................to windsurf

Ausgehen **Going out**

Willst du mitkommen?
Do you want to come with me?
die Begegnung (en) ......chance meeting
die Einladung (en) ....invitation
das Treffen (-) ....meeting
der Treffpunkt ....meeting place
die Verabredung (en)....date, appointment
der Vorschlag (-schläge)... suggestion

For **times** see page 8
For **days of the week** see page 8

Annehmen **Accepting**
Abgemacht ....OK, agreed
Danke schön ....Thank you
gern...............................with pleasure, gladly
gut.................................good
natürlich.........................of course
in Ordnung ....OK
sicher ....certainly
Es kommt darauf an .....It depends

Ablehnen **Refusing**
Es geht nicht, weil ... ..I can't, because ...
Es tut mir leid, aber ... Sorry, but ...
Ich kann nicht ....I can't
Ich bin verabredet.........I'm busy
Ich muss absagen..........I have to cancel
Ich habe keine Lust.......I don't feel like it

nein, danke................... no thank you
leider .... unfortunately

In die Stadt gehen **Going into town**
mit dem Auto............... by car
mit dem Bus................ by bus
mit dem Rad .... by bike
mit dem Taxi .... by taxi
mit dem Wagen .... by car
mit dem Zug .... by train

mit der Bahn .... by train
mit der S-Bahn............ on the local train
mit der Straßenbahn..... by tram
mit der U-Bahn .... on the underground
zu Fuß .... on foot

der Bahnhof (-höfe) ..... station
der Busbahnhof (-höfe)......bus station
die Bushaltestelle (n)... bus stop
die Buslinie (n) .... bus route
die Endstation (en)....... terminus
die einfache Fahrkarte . single ticket
der Fahrkartenautomat (en) *wk*
....ticket machine
der Fahrkartenschalter (-) .....ticket office
der Fahrplan (-pläne) ....timetable
die Hauptverkehrszeit (en) ...rush hour
die Rückfahrkarte (n)............return ticket
die Straßenbahnhaltestelle (n) .. tram stop
die Straßenbahnlinie (n) ....tram line
die U-Bahnstation (en)
.... underground station
die Verbindung (en).............connection

direkt........................... direct, through
gültig........................... valid
letzte .... last
nächste .... next

Treffpunkte **Meeting places**

der Ball (Bälle)............ball
das Café (s)..................café
die Disco (s)................disco
das Eiscafé (s)..............ice cream parlour
das Geschäft (e)...........shop
der Jugendklub (s)........youth club
das Jugendzentrum (-zentren) ...youth centre
das Kino (s).................cinema
der Laden (Läden)........shop
der Nachtklub (s)..........night club
der Park (s)..................park
die Party (s).................party (celebration)
das Restaurant (s).........restaurant
die Veranstaltung (en)...... show, event, do

die Eisbahn (en)...........ice rink
das Freibad (-bäder)......open air pool
das Hallenbad (-bäder)..... indoor pool
die Kegelbahn (en).......bowling alley
das Schwimmbad (-bäder)
...............................swimming pool
der Sportplatz (-plätze)..........sports ground
das Sportzentrum (-zentren)...sports centre
das Stadion (Stadien)....stadium
der Verein (e)...............club, society

der Ausflug (-flüge)......trip, outing
die Ausstellung (en).....exhibition
die Führung (en)...........guided tour
die Galerie (n).............art gallery
die Halle (n).................hall (public, sport)
das Konzert (e)............concert
das Spiel (e).................match
das Theater (-).............theatre
der Tiergarten (-gärten).....zoo
das Treffen (-)..............meeting

besuchen †...................to visit
einkaufen gehen* *irreg*.... to go shopping
in die Stadt gehen*.......to go to town
zum Flohmarkt gehen*
.....................to go to the flea market

nach Hause kommen* *irreg*
...............................to come back home
einen Einkaufsbummel machen
............................to go round the shops
einen Schaufensterbummel machen
............................to go window shopping
mitfahren* *irreg sep*.....to go with s.o
Schlange stehen *irreg*...to queue
sich treffen *irreg*..........to meet
das Haus verlassen *irreg*..to leave the house

ein Schloss besichtigen †
.... to visit a stately home
entwerten †...................to date-stamp ticket
Fotos machen................to take photos
einen Platz reservieren †..to book a seat

zum Gottesdienst gehen* *irreg*
................to go to (protestant) church
zur Messe gehen*.........to go to mass
zur Moschee gehen*.....to go to the mosque
zur Synagoge gehen* ...to go to synagogue

For **religion** see page 11
For **transport** see page 59
For **times** see page 8

Hobbys zu Hause **Hobbies at home**

die Aktivität (en)..........activity
das Basteln....................creative craft
das Fotografieren..........photography
die Freizeitbeschäftigung..hobby
das Hobby (s)................hobby
das Kochen...................cooking
die Lektüre....................reading
das Malen......................painting
der Modellbau...............model-making
die Musik......................music
das Nähen.....................sewing
das Zeichnen.................drawing

das Brettspiel (e)...........board game
das Damespiel...............draughts

die DVD (s) .... DVD
der Film (e) .... film
der Fotoapparat (e) .... camera
die Karten *pl* .... cards
das Kreuzworträtsel (-) . crossword
das Poster (-) .... poster
die Sammlung (en) .... collection
das Schach .... chess

sich amüsieren † .... to amuse o.s
sich ausruhen *sep* .... to rest
basteln .... to make models, do DIY
einen Film drehen .... to make a film
sich entspannen † .... to relax
Witze erzählen † .... to tell jokes
faulenzen † .... to laze about
fernsehen *irreg sep* .... to watch TV
sich interessieren für † (+ Acc)
.... to be interested in
malen .... to paint
modellieren † .... to make models (of clay, etc)
nähen .... to sew
sammeln .... to collect
Karten spielen .... to play cards
stricken .... to knit
zeichnen † .... to draw

Die Lektüre **Reading**

der Artikel (-) .... article
der Bericht (e) .... report
das Buch (Bücher) .... book
die Illustrierte (n) ‡ .... illustrated magazine
der Kriminalroman (e) ...... detective story
der Liebesroman (e) ...... love story
die Literatur .... literature
die Modezeitschrift (en) ... fashion magazine
der Roman (e) .... novel
der Science-Fiction-Roman (e)
.... sci-fi story
das Tagebuch (-bücher) diary
die Tageszeitung (en) .. daily paper
das Taschenbuch (-bücher) ... paperback
die Umfrage (n) .... survey
die Zeitschrift (en) .... magazine
die Zeitung (en) .... newspaper

das Ende .... end
die Handlung .... plot
der Held (en) *wk* .... hero
die Heldin (nen) .... heroine
die Leidenschaft (en) ... passion
die Rolle (n) .... role
die Seite (n) .... page
das Thema (Themen) ... theme

eine Art .... a sort of
das Ding (e) .... thing
das Dingsbums .... a thingummyjig
der Eindruck (e) .... impression
der Typ (en) .... type, fellow

informativ .... informative
lehrreich .... instructive

Es handelt sich um ….. It's about …
wünschen .... to wish
vorschlagen *irreg sep* .. to suggest

For **opinions** see page 10
For **internet** see page 45

SHOPPING, FASHION, TRENDS AND MONEY

Allgemeines **General**

das Einkaufen .... shopping
der Einkauf (Einkäufe)..... shopping
der Einkaufskorb .... shopping basket
die Einkaufsliste (n) ..... shopping list
die Einkaufstasche (n).. shopping bag
das Einkaufszentrum (-zentren) .... shopping centre
das Geschäft (e) .... shop
der Laden (Läden) .... shop
die Stadtmitte (n) .... town centre
der Stadtrand (-rände) .. outskirts
das Stadtzentrum .... town centre

Leute **People**

der Geschäftsführer (-) ....manager
die Geschäftsführerin (nen)....manager
der Händler (-).............. shopkeeper, trader
die Händlerin (nen) ...... shopkeeper, trader
der Kassierer (-)............ cashier
die Kassiererin (nen) .... cashier
der Kunde (n) *wk*.......... customer
die Kundin (nen) .... customer
der Verkäufer (-) .... sales assistant
die Verkäuferin (nen)... sales assistant

Die Geschäfte **The shops**

die Apotheke (n) .... chemist's shop (dispensing)
die Bäckerei (en) .... baker's shop
die Drogerie (n)............ chemist's shop (non-dispensing)
die Fleischerei .... butcher's shop
das Kaufhaus (-häuser)..... department store
die Konditorei (en)....... cake shop, sweet shop
das Lebensmittelgeschäft (e) ..grocer's shop
der Markt (Märkte)....... market
die Metzgerei (en)........ butcher's shop
der Supermarkt (-märkte).......supermarket
der Zeitungsstand (-stände)....news stand

der Blumenladen (-läden)...... flower shop
die Buchhandlung (en) .... bookshop
das Delikatessengeschäft (e).. delicatessen
die Gemüsehandlung (en)...... greengrocer's
das Kleidergeschäft (e) .... clothes shop
das Modegeschäft (e)............. boutique
die Obsthandlung (en) .... fruit seller's
die Reinigung .... dry cleaner's
das Schreibwarengeschäft (e) ....stationer's shop
der Tante-Emma-Laden (Läden) ....convenience store, corner shop

die Eisenwarenhandlung (en) ....ironmonger's shop
das Elektrogeschäft (e) ..... electrical shop
das Fischgeschäft (e).....fish shop
das Fotogeschäft (e)......photographer's
das Juweliergeschäft (e)....jeweller's shop
der Optiker (-)...............optician
das Reisebüro (s) ....travel agency
der Tabakwarenladen (-läden) ....tobacconist's shop
das Warenhaus (-häuser)... department store

Im Geschäft **In the shop**

das Erdgeschoss............ground floor
die Etage (n) ....storey
das Geschoss (-e)..........floor
der Eingang (-gänge) ....entrance
der Stock (Stockwerke) ... floor
der oberste Stock ....top floor
das Untergeschoss.........basement

die Abteilung (en) ....department
der Aufzug (-züge) ....lift
die Ausstellung (en) .....display
der Fahrstuhl (-stühle) ..lift
die Kasse (n).................cash desk
die Rolltreppe (n) ....escalator
das Schaufenster (-) ......shop window
die Umkleidekabine (n)... changing room

der Artikel (-) .... article
der Einkaufswagen (-) .. trolley
das Etikett (en) .... label
der Korb (Körbe) .... basket
die Marke (n) .... make, brand
der Pfand .... deposit (on bottle)
die Plastiktüte (n) .... plastic bag
der Preis (e) .... price
das Produkt (e) .... product
die Qualität (en) .... quality
die Quittung (en) .... receipt
die Waren *pl* .... goods

Schilder	**Signs**
Achtung!	Attention! Look out!
Anprobe	fitting room
Ausgang	exit
Ausverkauf	sale
ausverkauft	sold out
Drücken	push
Eingang	entrance
geöffnet	open
geschlossen	closed
Notausgang	emergency exit
Öffnungszeiten *pl*	opening hours
reduziert	reduced
Ruhetag	rest day
Schlussverkauf	(closing down) sale
Selbstbedienung	self-service
Sommerschlussverkauf	summer sale
Sonderangebot	on special offer
Winterschlussverkauf	winter sale
Ziehen	pull
zu verkaufen	for sale

an der Kasse bezahlen .. pay at the cash desk
aus zweiter Hand .... second-hand
bitte nicht berühren ...... please do not touch
hier erhältlich .... on sale here
Preisknüller .... fantastic prices
Preisliste .... price list
Preisnachlass .... reductions

Öffnungszeiten	**Opening times**
Geschäftszeiten	opening hours
an Feiertagen	on bank holidays
um ein Uhr	at one o'clock
eine halbe Stunde	half an hour
die Stunde (n)	hour, sixty minutes
(durchgehend) geöffnet	open (all day)
geschlossen	closed
von 9 Uhr bis 12 Uhr	from 9.00 till 12.00

Sachen kaufen	**Buying things**
die CD (s)	CD
der Computer (-)	computer
die DVD (s)	DVD
das Geschenk (e)	present
das Handy (s)	mobile phone
die Klamotten *pl (coll)*	clothes, stuff
die Kleider *pl*	clothes
die Turnschuhe *pl*	trainers
das Videospiel (e)	video-game
die Zeitschrift (en)	magazine

die Kosten *pl* .... expense, cost
die Marke (n) .... brand
die Markentreue .... brand loyalty

For **sports equipment** see page 35

Kleidung kaufen	**Buying clothes**
der Badeanzug (-züge)	swimsuit
die Badehose (n)	swimming trunks
die Bluse (n)	blouse
das Hemd (en)	shirt
die Hose (n)	pair of trousers
die Jacke (n)	jacket
die Jeans	pair of jeans
der Hut (Hüte)	hat
das Kleid (er)	dress
die Krawatte (n)	tie
der Mantel (Mäntel)	coat, overcoat
der Pulli (s) *coll*	pullover

der Pullover (-) .... pullover
der Regenmantel........... raincoat
der Rock (Röcke) .... skirt
der Sakko (s) .... jacket (man)
der Schlips (e) .... tie
die Shorts *pl* .... pair of shorts
das Sweatshirt (s) .... sweatshirt
das T-Shirt (s)............... T-shirt
der Trainingsanzug (-züge) ....tracksuit

der Hausschuh (e)......... slipper
ein Paar ... . a pair of ...
der Pantoffel (n) .... slipper
die Sandale (n) .... sandal
der Schuh (e) .... shoe
die Socke (n) .... sock
der Stiefel (-) .... boot
die Turnschuhe *pl*......... trainers

der Bademantel (-mäntel).. dressing gown
der BH (s).................... bra
der Büstenhalter (-) ...... bra
das Nachthemd (en)...... nightdress
der Schlafanzug (-anzüge)...pyjamas
der Slip (s)................... pants
die Strumpfhose (n) ..... tights
die Unterhose (n).......... underpants
die Unterwäsche........... underwear

der Bikini (s) .... bikini
der Gürtel (-) .... belt
der Handschuh (e) .... glove
der Hut (Hüte) .... hat
die Mütze (n)................ cap, hat
die Schürze (n) .... apron

der Anzug (Anzüge)..... suit (man)
der Hosenanzug............ trouser suit
das Kostüm (e) .... suit (with skirt)
der Schal (s) .... scarf
die Weste (n)................ waistcoat

das Armband (-bänder)...... bracelet
die Armbanduhr (en) ....watch
der Ärmel (-)................ sleeve
die Halskette (n) .... necklace
der Knopf (Knöpfe) ...... button
der Kragen (-) .... collar
der Modeschmuck .... costume jewellery
die Ohrringe *pl* .... earrings
der Regenschirm (e) ..... umbrella
der Reißverschluss (-schlüsse) ...zip
der Ring (e).................. ring
der Schmuck .... jewellery
die Tasche (n) .... pocket; bag
das Taschentuch (-tücher)... handkerchief

Make-up **Make-up**
der Lidschatten .... eye shadow
der Lippenstift (e) .... lipstick
die Mascara .... mascara
der Nagellack................ nail polish
das Parfüm .... perfume
die Schminke................ make-up
die Tätowierung (en) .... tattoo
sich schminken .... to put on make-up

Material **Material**
aus Baumwolle .... made of cotton
aus Gold .... made of gold
aus Leder .... made of leather
aus Seide....................... made of silk
aus Silber .... made of silver
aus Stoff .... made of cloth
aus Wolle....................... made of wool

aus Gummi .... made of rubber
aus Holz........................ made of wood
aus Kunststoff............... made of plastic
aus Metall .... made of metal
aus Stahl .... made of steel

Welche Größe? **What size are you?**
klein .... small
mittelgroß .... medium
groß .... large
Größe 40 .... size 12
der Meter .... metre
der Zentimeter .... centimetre

Welche Schuhgröße haben Sie?
What size shoes do you take?
Größe 38 .... size 5
Größe 42 .... size 8

Für wen ist es? **Who is it for?**
Es ist für mich .... It's for me
Es ist ein Geschenk ...... It's a present

Wie ist es? **What is it like?**
dunkel .... dark (colour)
gestreift .... striped
hell .... light (colour)
kariert .... check
kostbar, wertvoll .... valuable
uni *inv* .... plain coloured

zu eng .... too tight
zu groß .... too big
zu klein .... too small
zu kurz .... too short
zu teuer .... too expensive
zu weit .... too big, too wide

For **colours** see page 2

Trends **Trends**
das Mannequin (s) .... model (person)
die Mode (n) .... fashion
der Stil (e) .... style
die Tätowierung (en) .... tattoo

ähnlich .... similar
anders .... different
aus zweiter Hand .... second hand
billig .... cheap

eng .... tight-fitting
gratis .... free
günstig .... reasonably priced
komplett .... complete
kostenlos .... free
modisch .... fashionable
preiswert .... cheap, good value
verschieden .... different
unmodisch .... unfashionable
etwas Billigeres .... something cheaper

anprobieren † *sep* .... to try on
ausgeben *irreg sep* .... to spend
auswählen *sep* .... to choose
beweisen *irreg* .... to prove
bringen *irreg* .... to bring
einwickeln *sep* .... to wrap up, gift wrap
falten † .... to fold
messen *irreg* .... to measure
dran sein* *irreg* .... to be next (in queue)
versprechen *irreg* .... to promise
vorschlagen *irreg sep* .. to suggest
vorziehen *irreg sep* ...... to prefer
wiegen *irreg* .... to weigh
zurückkommen* *irreg sep* .... to come back

Bezahlen **Paying**
das Bargeld .... cash
der Cent .... cent
der Euro, € .... euro, €
der 20-Euro-Schein (e) ..... 20 euro note
das Geld .... money
das Geldstück (e) .... coin
das Kleingeld .... change
die Münze (n) .... coin
der Schein (e) .... note

die Bankkarte (n) .... bank card
die Brieftasche (n) .... wallet
die EC-Karte® (n) .... German debit card
der Geldautomat (en) *wk*... cash machine
der Geldbeutel (-) .... purse

die Kasse (n) .... cash desk, till
die Kreditkarte (n)........ credit card
die Mehrwertsteuer ...... VAT
die MwSt...................... VAT
das Portemonnaie (s) .... purse
der Preis (e) .... price
die Quittung (en).......... receipt
die Rechnung (en)........ bill, invoice
die Visa®-Karte (n) ..... Visa® card
das Wechselgeld........... change
die Zahlung (en)........... payment

das Stück, pro Stück..... each
je.................................. each
genau .... exact
Prozent .... per cent
an der Kasse bezahlen † ... to pay at the till

akzeptieren † .... to accept
Geld ausgeben *irreg sep*... to spend money
(zu viel) ausgeben .... to spend (too much)
bezahlen † .... to pay, pay for
brauchen....................... to need
an die Kasse gehen* *irreg*
.... to go to the cash desk
prüfen .... to check
rechnen † .... to add
schulden † .... to owe
unterschreiben *irreg insep*..... to sign
zusammenrechnen † *sep* .... to add up

Geld abheben *irreg sep* ... to withdraw cash
die Quittung aufheben *irreg sep*
.... to keep the receipt
ein Formular ausfüllen *sep*..... to fill in a form
die Quittung behalten *irreg*
.... to keep the receipt
Preise erhöhen *irreg* .... to raise prices
knapp bei Kasse sein* *irreg*.... to be broke
Geld zurückbekommen *irreg sep*
.... to get money back
Das reicht .... That's enough

Probleme **Problems**
die Batterie (n).............. battery
der Fleck (en)................ stain
die Garantie (n) .... guarantee, warranty
die Gebrauchsanweisung.. instructions
das Leck (s).................. leak
das Loch (Löcher)......... hole
das Missverständnis (se)... misunderstanding
die Reparatur (en)......... repair

defekt............................ broken, not working
eingelaufen .... shrunk
enttäuscht...................... disappointed
gebrochen .... broken
geklemmt...................... jammed, stuck
gerissen......................... torn
kaputt............................ broken, not working
pleite .... broke (no money)
praktisch .... practical
solide .... strong, solid
unzerbrechlich .... unbreakable
verschlissen .... worn out
zerbrechlich .... breakable
zerkratzt........................ scratched
(nicht) zufrieden ....(not) satisfied

abnutzen *sep* .... to wear out
austauschen *sep* .... to exchange
beschädigen † .... to damage
sich beschweren †......... to complain
einlaufen *irreg sep*........ to shrink
ersetzen † .... to replace
fallen lassen *irreg* .... to drop
funktionieren † .... to work, function
garantieren † .... to guarantee
kaputt gehen* *irreg* ...... to break
kontrollieren † .... to check
kritisieren †................... to criticise
liefern .... to supply
reinigen......................... to clean (personally)
reinigen lassen *irreg* ..... to have cleaned
reißen *irreg* .... to tear, rip

reparieren † .... to mend (personally)
reparieren † lassen *irreg* ... to have mended
umtauschen *sep* .... to change
zählen .... to count
Geld zurückgeben *irreg sep*
.... to refund money
zurücknehmen *irreg sep* ... to take back
Es ist mir gelungen .... I succeeded

Auf der Post **At the post office**
die Adresse (n) .... address
die Ansichtskarte (n) .... picture postcard
der Brief (e) .... letter
der Briefkasten (-kästen) .. letter box
die Briefmarke (n) .... stamp
der Briefträger (-) .... postman
das Formular (e)........... form
die nächste Leerung...... the next collection
das Päckchen (-)........... small parcel
das Paket (e) .... parcel
die Post......................... post office; mail
das Postamt (-ämter)..... post office
die Postanweisung (en) ..... postal order
die Postkarte (n) .... postcard
der Schalter (-).............. counter position
die postlagernde Sendung ..... poste restante
die Telefonkarte (n)...... phone card

ins Ausland.................. (to) abroad
per Einschreiben........... by registered post
per Luftpost .... by air mail

dringend .... urgent
verloren .... lost

benutzen † .... to use
einwerfen *irreg sep* ...... to post
sich irren .... to make a mistake
schicken .... to send, post
weiterschicken *sep* .... to send on
die Post zustellen *sep* ... to deliver the post

For **phoning** see page 89

In der Bank **At the bank**
die Bank (en) .... bank
der Geldwechsel .... exchange of money
die Sparkasse (n) .... savings bank
die Währung (en)......... currency

der Franken .... Swiss franc
der (Wechsel)Kurs .... rate of exchange
das Pfund .... £ sterling
der Rappen .... 100 = 1 Swiss franc
die Wechselstube (n) ... bureau de change

der Ausweis (e)........... ID
das Konto (s)................ account
der Pass (Pässe) .... passport

Provision nehmen *irreg*
.... to charge commission

For **paying** see page 42

NEW TECHNOLOGY - ADVANTAGES AND DISADVANTAGES

Informatik **ICT**

der Bildschirm (e) .... screen, monitor
der Computer (-).......... computer
der Cursor (s) .... cursor
die Datei (en)............... data-base, file
der Diskdrive (s).......... disk drive
der Drucker (-)............. printer
die E-Mail (s).............. email
die Festplatte (n) .... hard disk
die Maus (Mäuse) .... mouse
das Menü (s)................ menu
die SMS (-).................. text message
die Software .... computer software
die Tabelle (n)............. spreadsheet
die Tastatur (en)........... keyboard
die Taste (n) .... key (on keyboard)
die Textverarbeitung .... word processing

Das Internet **The internet**

der Anbieter (-)............ server
der Benutzername (n) *wk* ... user name
das (Foto)Blog (s)......... (photo)blog
der Browser (-) .... browser
das Chatroom (s) .... chat room
die E-Mail-Adresse (n) email address
die Homepage (s) .... home page
die Internetseite (n) ...... web page
das Kennwort (-wörter) .... password
das Netz .... (world wide) web
die Suchmaschine (n)... search engine
die Webseite (n) .... web page; web site
die Website (s) .... web site

der Blogger (-)............. blogger
der Internetbenutzer (-)..... internet user

digital .... digital
elektrisch .... electrical
elektronisch .... electronic
interaktiv .... interactive
online............................ online

technisch....................... technical
technologisch................ technological

aufmachen *sep* .... to open
bearbeiten † .... to edit
betätigen † .... to operate, use
drücken .... to print
klicken .... to click
laden † .... to load
löschen.......................... to erase
operieren † .... to operate
programmieren † .... to program
scannen .... to scan
nach oben scrollen .... to scroll up
nach unten scrollen....... to scroll down
speichern....................... to save
tippen .... to type, key in
twittern .... to twitter
zwitschern .... to twitter

Tragbare Geräte **Portable devices**

der BlackBerry™.......... BlackBerry™
das Handy (s) .... mobile phone
das iPhone™ (s)............ iPhone™
der Laptop (s) .... laptop (computer)
das Mobiltelefon (e)...... mobile phone
der MP3-/4-Player (-) ... MP3/4 player
das Navi-Gerät (e)......... sat nav

Vorteile **Advantages**
Man kann: **You can:**

eine Website besuchen ..... go on a website
bloggen .... blog
Karten buchen .... buy tickets
chatten .... chat online
Musik downloaden .... download music
Informationen finden.... find information
forschen .... do research
kommunizieren............. communicate
lernen .... study
Wikipedia® lesen .... read Wikipedia®

eine SMS schicken .... send a text
simsen .... text
online spielen .... play online
im Internet surfen .... surf the net

informativ .... informative
lehrreich .... instructive
ohne Abonnement .... without subscription
ohne Vertrag .... pay as you go
auf Wunsch .... on demand

Nachteile **Problems**
der Angreifer (-) .... attacker
die elterliche Aufsicht .. parental supervision
persönliche Daten .... personal data
der Datenraub .... identity theft
der Fremde ‡ .... stranger
der Hacker (s) .... hacker
der Internetbetrug (-trüge) .. scam
das Internetmobbing ..... cyberbullying
das trojanische Pferd (e) ... Trojan horse
der Reinfall (-fälle) .... scam

der Schutzlose ‡ .... vulnerable person
die Spammail .... spam
die Verletzung der Privatsphäre
.... invasion of privacy
der Virus (Viren) .... (computer) virus

anziehend .... seductive
bösartig .... malicious
potentiell .... potential

jemanden abzocken *sep coll*
.... to rip someone off
belästigen † .... to pester
belästigt werden *irreg* .. to be pestered
betrügen *irreg* .... to rip someone off
schaffen .... to manage, get done
wissen, was die Kinder machen
.... to know what the children are doing
zielen .... to target

For **opinions** see page 10

HOLIDAYS

Die Unterkunft **Lodging**

der Anmeldezettel (-) ... registration form
der Campingplatz (-plätze).....camp site
die Ferienwohnung (en) ... holiday home
das Hotel (s) .... hotel
die Jugendherberge (n)..... youth hostel
die Pension (en) .... boarding house

Fremdenzimmer .... room available
Luxus- .... luxury
Halbpension .... half board
Vollpension .... full board
Zimmer frei .... room available

bequem .... comfortable
besetzt .... taken, occupied
frei .... available
(nicht) gestattet............ (not) allowed
(nicht) inbegriffen .... (not) included
luxuriös .... luxurious
privat .... private
voll .... full
übernachten † *insep*...... to stay the night

Die Überfahrt **Crossing the Channel**

der Ärmelkanal............ English Channel
die (Auto)Fähre (n) ...... (car) ferry
der Fährhafen (-häfen)...... ferry terminal
der Hafen (Häfen) .... port, harbour
die Hafenstadt (-städte).... port (town)
der Kanaltunnel .... Channel Tunnel
das Meer (e)................. sea
das Schiff (e) .... ship
die Überfahrt (en)......... crossing

glatt .... smooth
seekrank .... seasick
stürmisch .... rough (crossing)
an Bord .... on board
an Deck gehen* *irreg*... to go up on deck

Das Flugreisen **Flying**

der Billigflieger (-) ....low cost airline
der Flughafen (-häfen)...... airport
der Flugplatz (-plätze) ..(small) airport
das Flugzeug (e)...........plane
der Jumbojet (s)...........jumbo jet
die Kabine (n)..............cabin
die Maschine (n)..........plane

der Abflug (Abflüge)....departure
der Anflug (Anflüge)....arrival
die Ansage (n) ....call
die Autovermietung......car hire
der Flug (Flüge)...........flight
der Fluggast (-gäste).....passenger
der Flugsteig (e)...........gate
die Gepäckrückgabe .....baggage return
das Handgepäck ....hand luggage
die Landung (en) ....landing
der Passagier (e) ....passenger
die Passkontrolle ....passport control
die Pünktlichkeit ....punctuality
der Sicherheitsgurt (e) ..seat belt
die Sicherheitskontrolle.... airport security
der Scanner ....scanner
die Touristenklasse.......tourist class
der Treffpunkt..............meeting point
die Verspätung (en) ......delay
mit Verspätung ....delayed
schwer..........................heavy
verspätet ....delayed

abfliegen* *irreg sep*......to depart (plane)
bestätigen †...................to confirm
einchecken *sep*.............to check in
einen Platz finden *irreg*.... to find a seat
fliegen* *irreg*................to fly (person)
kontrollieren † ....to examine, check
landen* † ....to land
starten* † ....to take off (plane)

Mit dem Auto fahren Going by car

die Autobahn (en).........motorway
die Bundesstraße (en)...main road
die Landstraße (n) ....secondary road

die Ampel.....................traffic lights
die Ausfahrt..................motorway exit
das Autobahndreieck ....motorway interchange
das Autobahnkreuz (e)... motorway interchange
das Autobahnnetz ....motorway network
die Baustelle (n) ....roadworks
der Bürgersteig (e)........pavement
der Gehsteig (e) ....pavement
die Kreuzung (en).........crossroads
die Kurve (n) ....bend
die Maut (en)................toll
das Parkhaus (-häuser)
...............................multi-storey car park
der Parkplatz (-plätze)...... car park
der Rasthof (-höfe) ....service area
der Rastplatz (-plätze) ...... picnic area
die Raststätte (n)...........service area
der Stau (s) ....traffic jam, delay
das Straßenschild (er) ...road sign
die Tankstelle (n) ....petrol station
die Tiefgarage (n).........underground car park
die Toilette (n)..............toilet
die Umleitung (en) ....diversion
der Verkehrskreisel (-)...... roundabout

die Autowäsche ....car wash
das Ende (n).................end
die Fahrschule (n).........driving school
der Führerschein (e)......driving licence
die Gefahr (en) ....danger
die Geschwindigkeit (en) .... speed
die Hauptverkehrszeit (en)........ rush hour
die Landkarte (n) ....map
die Lebensgefahr ....danger of death
die Rückfahrt (en) ....return journey
die Straßenkarte (n)......map
die Straßenverkehrsordnung.... highway code
die Vorfahrt..................right of way, priority

die Werkstatt (-stätten)......garage (repairs)

abbiegen* *irreg sep* ..... to turn (off road)
bremsen .... to brake
fahren* *irreg* (+ sein)... to travel, go
fahren *irreg* (+ haben) . to drive (a vehicle)
rückwärts fahren* *irreg*.....to reverse
parken .... to park
überholen *insep*........... to overtake
überqueren *insep*......... to cross
volltanken *sep*............. to fill up with fuel

den Motor anlassen *irreg sep*
.... to start the engine
die Scheinwerfer anmachen *sep*
.... to switch on headlights
eine Panne haben *irreg*.....to break down
die Reifen nachsehen *irreg sep*
.... to check the tyres
am Steuer sitzen *irreg*.......to sit at the wheel
die Windschutzscheibe waschen *irreg*
.... to wash the windscreen

Einfahrt freihalten........ keep entrance clear

Am Meer At the seaside

die Ebbe...................... low tide
die Flut........................ high tide
die Klippe (n).............. cliff
die Küste (n) .... coast
die Möwe (n) .... seagull
die Muschel (n)........... shell
der Sand .... sand
der Schlamm .... mud
die See (n).................. sea
der Strand (Strände)..... beach
die Welle (n)............... wave (sea)

der Badeort (e) .... seaside resort
das Boot (e)................. boat
das Eis......................... ice cream
der Eisverkäufer (-)...... ice cream seller
der Fischer (-) .... fisherman
der Hafen (Häfen)........ port
der Kai (s) .... quay

der Kutter (-) .... fishing boat
der Leuchtturm (-türme)... lighthouse
der Nachtklub (s).......... night club
der Rettungsring (e)...... lifebelt
das Ruderboot (e) .... rowing boat
das Schlauchboot (e) .... inflatable dinghy
das Segelboot (e) .... dinghy
der (un)überwachte Strand
.... (un)supervised beach
das Surfbrett (er).......... surfboard

die Angelrute (n) .... fishing rod
der Eimer (-)................. bucket
die Sonnenbrille (n) ..... sunglasses
der Sonnenhut (-hüte)... sunhat
das Sonnenöl .... sun oil
der Spaten (-)................ spade
der Strandkorb (-körbe)
.... wicker wind-break and seat

baden † .... to bathe
rudern .... to row
schwimmen (*) *irreg*.... to swim, bathe
segeln .... to sail
sich sonnen................... to sunbathe
spazieren gehen* *irreg*..... to go for a walk
surfen............................ to surf
tauchen* .... to dive
windsurfen.................... to windsurf

Wintersport **Winter sports**
der Berg (e) .... mountain
die Eisbahn (en) .... ice rink
der Gletscher (-) .... glacier
der Hang (Hänge)......... slope
die Hütte (n) .... mountain refuge
die Lawine (n) .... avalanche
die Piste (n) .... piste, ski run
der Schnee .... snow
die Seilbahn (en) .... cable car
die Sesselbahn (en) ...... chair lift
das Snowboarden.......... snowboarding
der Wintersportort (e)... ski resort

Leute **People**
der Anfänger (-)............ beginner
der Skiführer (-)............ ski guide
der Skilehrer (-) .... ski instructor
der Skifahrer (-) .... skier

Skiausrüstung **Skiing equipment**
der Handschuh (e) .... glove
die Mütze (n) .... hat
die Skibrille (n) .... ski goggles
die Skier *pl* .... skis
die Skihose (n).............. salopettes
die Skistiefel *pl*............. ski boots
der Skistock (-stöcke)... ski pole

Schlitten fahren* *irreg* ..... to go sledging
Ski fahren* *sep irreg*.... to ski
Ski laufen* *sep irreg*.... to ski
Snowboard fahren**irreg* .. to go snowboarding
Winterurlaub machen ... to take a winter holiday

For **opinions** see page 10
For **outings** see page 59
For **weather** see page 12

Das Hotel **The hotel**
das Doppelzimmer (-)... double room
das Einzelzimmer (-) .... single room
das Familienzimmer (-) .... family room
der Preis (e) .... price
die Übernachtung (en)...... overnight stay
das Zimmer (-) .... room

die Anmeldung............. reception
der Ausgang (-gänge) ... exit
das Badezimmer (-) ...... bathroom
der Balkon (s) .... balcony
der Eingang (-gänge) .... entrance
der Empfang (-fänge) ... reception
das Erdgeschoss .... ground floor
der Fahrstuhl (-stühle) .. lift
der Keller (-) .... basement

der Notausgang (-gänge) .. emergency exit
der Parkplatz (-plätze) ...... car park
das Restaurant (s) .... restaurant
die Rezeption................ reception
der Stock (Stöcke) .... storey
die Toiletten *pl* .... toilets
die Treppe (n)............... stairs
das Treppenhaus (-häuser)
.... staircase, stairwell

Leute **People**
die Empfangsdame (n) ..... receptionist
der Geschäftsführer (-) ..... manager
der Inhaber (-)............... owner
der Kellner (-)............... waiter
die Kellnerin (nen) .... waitress
das Zimmermädchen (-)..... chambermaid

Das Schlafzimmer **Bedroom**
das Bad .... bath
das Bett (en).................. bed
die Bettdecke (n) .... blanket
das (Bett)Tuch (-tücher) ... sheet
das Bettzeug *no pl* .... bedding
das Doppelbett (en)....... double bed
die Dusche (n) .... shower
das Etagenbett (en) .... bunk bed
der Fernsehapparat (e) .. TV set
der Fernseher (-) .... TV set
das Fernsehgerät (e)...... TV set
das Handtuch (-tücher) ..... towel
der Internetanschluss .... internet connection
der Kleiderbügel (-)...... coathanger
der Kleiderschrank (-schränke) ..... wardrobe
das Kopfkissen (-)......... pillow
das Laken (-)................ sheet
der Schlüssel (-)............ key
die Seife........................ soap
die Steppdecke (n)........ duvet, quilt
das Telefon (e).............. telephone
die Wolldecke (n)......... blanket

Der Campingplatz **The campsite**
das Camping .... camping
das Camping Carnet (s)...... camping carnet
der Empfang .... reception
das Fahrzeug (e)........... vehicle
das Freibad (-bäder)..... open air pool
die Sanitäranlage (n).... toilet block
das Schwimmbad (bäder)... swimming pool
das Spielzimmer................. games room
der Stellplatz (-plätze) .... pitch
der Waschraum (-räume)... washroom
der Wohnwagen (-)...... caravan
das Zelt (e) .... tent
der Zuschlag (Zuschläge)... supplement

der elektrische Anschluss .. electric hook-up
das Spülbecken (-) .... washing up sink
die Wäscherei .... laundry
warmes Essen zum Mitnehmen
.... hot take-away meals

die Campingausrüstung
.... camping equipment
der Campingkocher (-)...... camping stove
der Klappstuhl (-stühle).... folding chair
der Klapptisch (e) .... folding table
die Lebensmittel *pl*...... food(stuff)
die Luftmatratze (n)..... air bed
der Schlafsack (-säcke)..... sleeping bag
die Streichhölzer *pl*...... matches
die Taschenlampe (n) .. torch
das Taschenmesser (-).. pocket knife

Keine Lagerfeuer .... no camp fires
der Radverleih............. cycle hire
(Kein) Trinkwasser...... (non) drinking water
die Wäsche .... washing (clothes)
die Waschmaschine (n) ..... washing machine

im Freien..................... in the open air
im Schatten .... shady
in der Sonne................ sunny

ein Zelt abbauen *sep*.....to take down tent
ein Zelt aufschlagen *irreg sep*....to put up tent
campen ....to camp
grillen ....to barbecue, grill
zelten † ....to camp

Die Jugendherberge Youth hostel
der Aufenthaltsraum (-räume) ....day room
das Büro (s) ....office
die DJH ....German youth hostel
der Fernsehraum (-räume).....TV room
die Küche (n)................kitchen
der Schlafraum (-räume) .. dormitory
der Speisesaal (-säle)........ dining room
der Tagesraum (-räume)... day room

der Abfalleimer (-) ....rubbish bin
die Bettwäsche ....sheets, bed linen
die Decke (n)...............blanket
der Leinenschlafsack (-säcke) ....sheet sleeping bag

die Nachtruhe ....night-time silence
heißes Wasser..............hot water
kaltes Wasser ....cold water

bezahlen † ....to pay
buchen ....to book
mieten †........................to hire
reservieren †................to reserve, book
unterschreiben *irreg insep*...to sign

For **food** see page 17
For **restaurant** see page 55
For **weather** see page 12
For **holiday activities** see page 47
For **days, months, seasons** see page 8, 9
For **lodging** see page 47

Leute People
der Besitzer (-).............owner
der Busfahrer (-)..........coach driver
der Camper (-) ....camper
die Empfangsdame (n) .....receptionist
die Herbergseltern *pl* .... youth hostel wardens (couple)
die Herbergsmutter.......youth hostel warden
der Herbergsvater ....youth hostel warden
der Reiseleiter (-).........group leader, courier
der Reisende ‡ ....traveller
der Tourist (en) *wk* ....tourist
die Touristin (nen)........tourist
der Urlauber (-)............holiday maker

Einen Austausch mitmachen Going on an exchange
der Brieffreund (e)........penfriend
die Brieffreundin (nen).....penfriend
die Brieffreundschaft....penfriendship
die deutsche Familie.....German family
die englische Familie....English family
der Lehrer (-) ....teacher
die Lehrerin (nen).........teacher

der Ausflug (-flüge)......trip, outing
die Dauer ....length (stay, lesson)
das Fahrgeld.................travel money
die Freizeit....................free time
die Hausaufgaben *pl*.....homework
die deutsche Küche ......German cooking
die englische Küche .....English cooking
die Partnerstadt (-städte) ..twin town
die Reise (n) ....journey
die Schule (n) ....school
die Schuluniform..........school uniform
die Sitte (n)..................customs, habits
der Sport ....sport
die Städtepartnerschaft..... town twinning
die Stunden..................lessons
das Taschengeld...........pocket money
der Vergleich (e)..........comparison

Herzlich willkommen! ..... Welcome!
Schöne Grüße!.............Greetings!
Gute Reise!..................Have a good journey

auspacken *sep* .... to unpack (suitcase)
besuchen † .... to visit
einpacken *sep* .... to pack (suitcase)
Heimweh haben *irreg* ... to be homesick
kontaktieren † .... to contact
organisieren † .... to arrange, organise
packen .... to pack (suitcase)
vergleichen *irreg* mit (+ Dat)
.... to compare with

For **opinions** see page 10
For **holidays** see page 47
For **special occasions** see page 76
For **restaurants** see page 55

Als Gast **Being a guest**
der Gast (Gäste) .... guest (m)
die Gastfreundschaft ..... hospitality
der Gastgeber (-) .... host
die Gastgeberin (nen) ... hostess

das Geschenk (e) .... present
der Koffer (-) .... suitcase
die Reisetasche (n) .... holdall
die Seife .... soap
das Shampoo .... shampoo
die Wolldecke (n) .... blanket
die Zahnbürste (n) .... toothbrush
die Zahnpasta .... toothpaste

englisch .... English
irisch .... Irish
schottisch .... Scottish
walisisch .... Welsh

belgisch .... Belgian
deutsch .... German
luxemburgisch .... Luxembourgish
österreichisch .... Austrian
schweizerisch .... Swiss

Ich bin Engländer .... I am English
Ich bin Engländerin ..... I am English
Ich bin Ire .... I am Irish
Ich bin Irin .... I am Irish
Ich bin Schotte .... I am Scottish
Ich bin Schottin .... I am Scottish
Ich bin Waliser .... I am Welsh
Ich bin Waliserin .... I am Welsh

älter .... older, elder
dankbar .... thankful, grateful
freundlich .... welcoming, friendly
jünger .... younger
schüchtern .... shy
verantwortlich .... responsible
willkommen .... welcome

abfahren* *irreg sep* ...... to leave, depart
ankommen* *irreg sep* .. to arrive
ausgehen* *irreg sep* ..... to go out
ausleihen *irreg sep* .... to borrow, to lend
begrüßen † .... to greet
besuchen † .... to visit
brauchen .... to need
danken (+ Dat) .... to thank
empfangen *irreg* .... to receive (guest)
helfen *irreg* (+ Dat) ..... to help
lächeln .... to smile
leihen *irreg* .... to lend
schenken .... to give (present)
sprechen *irreg* .... to speak
Deutsch sprechen *irreg* .... to speak German
Englisch sprechen *irreg* ...... to speak English
teilen .... to share
Fotos zeigen .... to show photos
verstehen *irreg* .... to understand
wiedersehen *irreg sep* .... to see again
willkommen heißen *irreg* .. to welcome

For **holiday plans** see page 53

PLANS, PREFERENCES, EXPERIENCES

Allgemeines **General**

das Hotelverzeichnis (se).. list of hotels
das Informationsbüro (s) .. tourist office
die Preisliste (n) .... price list
das Reisebüro (s) .... travel agency
das Verkehrsamt (-ämter)...... tourist office
die Vorliebe (n) .... preference

der Aufenthalt (e) .... stay
die Aufenthaltsdauer .... length of stay
die Fahrt (en)................ journey
die Ferien *pl* .... holidays
die Gegend (en)........... region, area
das Land (Länder)......... country, state
die Region (en)............ region
die Reise (n) .... journey

das Ereignis (se) .... event
die Erinnerung (en) ...... memory
das Erlebnis (se) .... experience

erfüllen † .... to fulfil
erleben † .... to experience

Wohin? **Where to?**

ins Ausland.................. abroad
in die Berge .... to the mountains
auf das Land .... to the country
zum See .... to the lake
zum Strand .... to the beach

Wo? **Where?**

im Ausland .... abroad
in den Bergen .... in the mountains
auf dem Land .... in the country
am Strand .... at the beach

besichtigen † .... to visit (attraction)
in Urlaub fahren* *irreg* ..... to go on holiday
auf Urlaub sein* *irreg* .... to be on holiday
einen Ausflug machen....... to go for a trip
packen .... to pack

Wann? **When are you going?**

zu Weihnachten .... at Christmas
zu Ostern .... at Easter
im August .... in August
morgen.......................... tomorrow
übermorgen.................. the day after tomorrow
nächste Woche .... next week
in einer Woche .... in a week's time
in drei Monaten .... in three months' time
nächstes Jahr................ next year
in der Zukunft.............. in the future
im Frühling.................. in spring
im Sommer .... in summer
im Herbst .... in the autumn
im Winter .... in winter

Mit wem? **With whom?**

mit meiner Familie .... with my family
mit meinem Freund ...... with my friend (male)
mit meiner Freundin ..... with my friend (female)
mit meinen Freunden.... with my friends

Wie viele Personen? **For how many?**

der Erwachsene (n) ‡ .... adult
der Junge (n) *wk* .... boy
das Kind (er) .... child
das Mädchen (-) .... girl
die Person (en)............. person
bis drei Jahre .... under three years old

Für wie lange? **For how long?**

für einen Tag .... for a day
für einen Monat .... for a month
für eine Nacht .... for a night
für eine Woche .... for a week
für drei Tage .... for three days
für vier Nächte............. for four nights
für zwei Wochen .... for a fortnight

Wie ist es? **What is it like?**

beliebt.......................... popular
bildschön .... picturesque

einmalig .... unforgettable, unique
friedlich .... peaceful
historisch .... historic
hübsch .... pretty
sehenswert .... worth seeing
touristisch .... popular with tourists

Ich brauche ... **I need ...**
eine Broschüre .... a brochure
Fotos .... photos
einen Fotoapparat .... a camera
Geld .... money
einen Koffer .... a case
eine Krankenversicherungskarte .. EHIC
eine Landkarte .... a map
eine Mitgliedskarte .... a membership card
einen (Reise)Pass .... a passport
einen Rucksack .... a rucksack
eine Sonnenbrille .... sunglasses
einen Stadtplan .... a town plan
einen Studentenausweis ... NUS student card
eine Videokamera .... a camcorder

Zu vermieten **For hire**
der Ausweis .... identity card
das Boot (e) .... boat
das Fahrrad (-räder) ...... bike
der Fahrradverleih .... bike hire
die Kaution .... deposit
das Rad (Räder) .... bicycle

mieten † .... to hire
Unterschreiben Sie hier! ... sign here

Wann war das? **When did you go?**
am Wochenende .... at the weekend
in den Sommerferien .... in the summer holidays
letzte Woche .... last week
vor zwei Wochen .... a fortnight ago
vor zwei Monaten .... two months ago
letztes Jahr .... last year

Ich kaufte ... **I bought ...**
ein Andenken .... a souvenir
Ansichtskarten .... postcards
Aufkleber .... stickers
Kekse .... biscuits
Pralinen .... chocolates
eine Puppe .... a doll
einen Schlüsselring ...... a key ring
einen Schokoriegel ...... a chocolate bar
Souvenirs .... souvenirs
Süßwaren .... sweets
ein T-Shirt .... a T-shirt

Essen und Trinken Schilder **Eating and drinking Signs**
durchgehend warme Küche ... hot food all day
Erfrischungen .... refreshments
Tagesgericht .... dish of the day
Tagesmenü .... day's set price menu
zum Mitnehmen .... take-away

Ausrufe **Exclamations**
Fräulein! .... Waitress!
Herr Ober! .... Waiter!
Guten Appetit! .... Enjoy your meal!
Mahlzeit! .... Enjoy your meal!
Prost! .... Cheers!
Zum Wohl! .... Cheers!
Ich bin satt .... I've eaten enough
(nein) danke .... (no) thank you
Zahlen bitte! .... The bill, please

Die Mahlzeiten **Meals**
das Abendbrot (e) .... evening meal (cold)
das Abendessen (-) .... dinner, evening meal
das Frühstück (e) .... breakfast
der Imbiss (-e) .... snack
Kaffee und Kuchen ...... afternoon coffee and cake
das Mittagessen (-) .... lunch, midday meal
das Picknick (s) .... picnic

Wo kann man essen? Where can you eat?

die Bar (s) .... bar
das Café (s) .... café
der Erfrischungsstand ... snack bar
das Gasthaus (-häuser) .. pub, inn
der Gasthof (-höfe) .... pub, inn
die Gaststätte (n) .... pub
die Imbisshalle (n) .... snack bar
die Imbissstube (n) .... snack bar
die Kneipe (n) .... pub
die Konditorei (en) .... café; cake shop
das Lokal (e) .... pub
der Ratskeller (-) .... town hall cellar restaurant
das Restaurant (s) .... restaurant
der Schnellimbiss (-e) .. snack bar
das Stehcafé (s) .... quick café
die Theke (n) .... bar (in pub)
die Weinstube (n) .... wine bar
die Wirtschaft (en) .... pub
das Wirtshaus (-häuser) .... country pub
die Wurstbude (n) .... sausage stand
mit Stimmung .... with atmosphere

Leute People

der Gast (Gäste) .... guest
der Inhaber (-) .... owner
der Kassierer (-) .... till operator
der Kellner (-) .... waiter
die Kellnerin (nen) .... waitress
der Koch (Köche) .... cook, chef
die Köchin (nen) .... cook, chef
der Kunde (n) *wk* .... customer
die Kundin (nen) .... customer
die Serviererin (en) ...... waitress

Im Restaurant In a restaurant

am Fenster .... by the window
auf der Terrasse .... on the terrace
der Tisch (e) .... table
die Toiletten *pl* .... toilets

draußen .... outside
drinnen .... inside

die Auswahl .... choice
die britische Küche .... British food
die deutsche Küche ...... German food
die italienische Küche .. Italian food
die Spezialität (en) .... speciality

der Geruch (Gerüche) ... smell
der Geschmack (Geschmäcke) .... taste, flavour
die Portion (en) .... portion

die Bedienung .... service, service charge
die MwSt .... VAT
die Quittung (en) .... receipt
die Rechnung (en) .... bill
das Trinkgeld (er) .... tip (money)
der Zettel (-) .... chit

(nicht) inbegriffen .... (not) included
inbegr/einschl/inkl .... included
lecker .... tasty

Die Speisekarte Menu

das Gericht (e) .... dish
die Getränkekarte (n) .... drinks menu
das Hauptgericht (e) ...... main course
der Nachtisch (e) .... dessert
die Tageskarte (n) .... menu of the day
die Vorspeise (n) .... starter
die Weinkarte (n) .... wine list

Die Vorspeisen Starters

der Aufschnitt .... mixed cold meats
die Hühnerbrühe .... chicken soup
die Leberwurst .... liver sausage
die Pastete (n) .... vol-au-vent
die kalte Platte .... mixed cold meats
die Suppe (n) .... soup
der Tomatensalat (e) ..... tomato salad
die Wurst (Würste) .... salami, sausage

Das Hauptgericht	**Main course**
der Braten	roast meat
das Brathähnchen (-)	roast chicken
der Eintopf (Eintöpfe)	casserole, stew
das Kalbschnitzel (-)	veal escalope
das Kotelett (s)	chop, cutlet
das Omelett (s)	omelette
die Pizza (s)	pizza
der Rinderbraten	roast beef
der Sauerbraten	pickled roast beef
das Schweinekotelett (s)	pork chop
das Steak (s)	steak
das Wiener Schnitzel (-)	escalope in breadcrumbs

Gemüse	**Vegetables**
die Bratkartoffeln *pl*	fried potatoes
die Bohnen *pl*	beans
die Erbsen *pl*	peas
die Kartoffeln *pl*	potatoes
das Kartoffelpüree	mashed potatoes
die Pommes (Frites) *pl*	chips
der Reis	rice
der Salat	salad
die Salzkartoffeln *pl*	boiled potatoes

Der Nachtisch	**Dessert**
der Apfelkuchen (-)	apple tart, apple cake
der Apfelstrudel (-)	apple strudel
der Eisbecher	ice cream sundae
der Joghurt (s)	yoghurt
der Käsekuchen (-)	cheesecake
das Kompott	stewed fruit
der Kuchen (-)	gateau
der Obstsalat	fruit salad
der Pudding (-)	cold milk dessert
die Schlagsahne	whipped cream
das Schokoladeneis	chocolate ice cream
die Torte (n)	gateau, flan
das Vanilleeis	vanilla ice cream

Auf dem Tisch	**On the table**
der Becher (-)	mug
das Besteck	cutlery
die Flasche (n)	bottle
die Gabel (n)	fork
das Geschirr	crockery
das Glas (Gläser)	glass
die Kaffeekanne (n)	coffee pot
der Teelöffel (n)	teaspoon
der Korkenzieher (-)	corkscrew
der Krug (Krüge)	jug
der Löffel (-)	spoon
das Messer (-)	knife
der Pfeffer	pepper (spice)
das Salz	salt
die Schale (n)	bowl (shallow)
die Schüssel (n)	bowl (deep)
die Serviette (n)	serviette, napkin
die Tasse (n)	cup
das Tablett (s)	tray
die Teekanne (n)	teapot
der Teller (-)	plate
die Tischdecke (n)	tablecloth
die Untertasse (n)	saucer

Im Café — **In the café**

Getränke	**Drinks**
der Apfelsaft	apple juice
das Bier (vom Fass)	(draught) beer
die Cola	cola
der Kaffee	coffee
der Kakao	cocoa
das Kännchen (-)	individual pot
die Limo (s)	lemonade
die Limonade (n)	lemonade
das Mineralwasser	mineral water
der Orangensaft (-säfte)	orange juice
das Pils	lager
der Rotwein (e)	red wine
der Saft (Säfte)	fruit juice
der Schnaps	spirits
die Schokolade	chocolate

der Sprudel .... fizzy water; lemonade
der Tee.......................... tea
der Wein (e) .... wine
der Weißwein (e)......... white wine
der Zitronentee .... lemon tea

Der Imbiss **A snack**
der Berliner.................. doughnut
die Bockwurst (-würste).... frankfurter
die Bratwurst (-würste) ..... fried sausage
ein belegtes Brot .... open sandwich
das Butterbrot (e).......... sandwich
die Chips *pl* .... crisps
die Currywurst (-würste)... curried sausage
das Ei (er) .... egg
ein hart gekochtes Ei.... hard boiled egg
das Eis .... ice cream
die Frikadelle (n).......... large meatball
die Fritten *pl*................ chips
das Gebäck *no pl* .... biscuits
der Hamburger (-) .... beefburger
das Jägerschnitzel
.... escalope with mushroom sauce
das Käsebrot (e)........... cheese sandwich
der Kaugummi............. chewing gum
der Ketchup .... tomato ketchup
die Mayonnaise .... mayonnaise
die Pommes (Frites) *pl*...... chips
das Rührei..................... scrambled egg
der Schaschlik (s) .... kebab
das Schinkenbrot (e)..... ham sandwich
der Senf .... mustard
das Spiegelei................ fried egg
das Toastbrot (e).......... toast
die Waffel (n).............. waffle (edible)
das Würstchen (-) .... small sausage
das Zigeunerschnitzel
.... escalope with paprika sauce

Nützliche Verben **Useful verbs**
bestellen † .... to order
zu Abend essen *irreg* ... to have evening meal
zu Mittag essen *irreg* ... to have lunch
frühstücken .... to have breakfast
Durst haben *irreg* .... to be thirsty
Hunger haben *irreg* ...... to be hungry
kosten † .... to cost
lieben .... to love
probieren † .... to try
reservieren † .... to reserve
riechen *irreg* .... to smell
schmecken .... to taste
servieren † .... to serve
wählen .... to choose
durstig werden* *irreg*... to get thirsty
hungrig werden* *irreg*...... to get hungry

anbieten *irreg sep* .... to offer
bedienen † .... to serve
sich beklagen † .... to complain
empfehlen *irreg* .... to recommend
hassen .... to hate
reichen .... to pass
vorziehen *irreg sep*....... to prefer

For **accepting and refusing** see page 36
For **food** see page 17

Fundsachen **Lost property**
die Brille....................... pair of glasses
die Brieftasche (n) .... wallet
der Fotoapparat (e) .... camera
das Fundbüro (s) .... lost property office
die Handtasche (n)........ handbag
das Handy (s) .... mobile (phone)
der Koffer (-) .... suitcase
der MP3-Player (-)........ MP3 player
der Laptop (s) .... laptop (computer)
das Portemonnaie (s) .... purse
der Regenschirm (e) ..... umbrella
der Rucksack (-säcke) .. rucksack
der Schlüssel (-)........... key
der Schlüsselbund (e) ... bunch of keys
die Videokamera (s) ..... camcorder

die Belohnung (en).......reward
die Beschreibung (en) ..description
das Datum (Daten)........date
die Farbe (n) ....colour
das Formular (e)...........form
die Gebühr (en) ....fee
die Größe.....................size
die Marke (n)................make, brand
der Schaden (Schäden).....damage

eine Art.........................a sort of
Das gehört mir.............It's mine
Es gibt ... drin ....There is ... in it
verloren ....lost
zufällig..........................by chance

ausfüllen *sep*................to fill in (form)
berichten † ....to report
bieten *irreg*...................to offer
fallen lassen *irreg*.........to drop
liegen lassen *irreg* ....to leave behind
legen ....to put (down flat)
stecken..........................to put (in something)
stehlen *irreg* ....to steal
stellen ....to put (upright)
suchen...........................to look for
vergessen *irreg* ....to forget,
leave behind
verlieren *irreg*...............to lose

For **days of week** see page 8
For **colours** see page 2
For **materials** see page 41
For **forms of transport** see page 59

Ich habe eine Panne
My car has broken down

der Abschleppwagen ....breakdown truck
der ADAC ....breakdown service
der Notruf (e)................emergency call
die Panne (n) ....breakdown
der Pannendienst ....breakdown service

der Autoschlüssel (-).... car key
die Batterie (n)............ battery
das Benzin.................... petrol
die Bremse (n) .... brake
der Diesel..................... diesel
das Geräusch (e)........... noise (quiet-ish)
der Kühler (-) .... radiator
der Lärm .... noise (loud)
die Marke (n) .... make
der Motor (en)............. engine
das Öl .... oil
der Reifen (-) .... tyre
die Reifenpanne (n) ..... puncture
der Scheinwerfer (-)..... headlight
die Windschutzscheibe (n) .... windscreen

der Auspuff................. exhaust pipe
der Blinker (-) .... indicator
das Ersatzteil (e) .... spare part
das Gas(pedal)............. accelerator
die Hupe (n)................ horn
der Kofferraum (-räume) ..boot
die Kupplung (en)........ clutch
das Lenkrad (-räder)..... steering wheel
das Reserverad (-räder).....spare wheel
die Scheibe (n)............ window
die Scheibenwischer *pl*.....windscreen wipers
die Schlussleuchten *pl* ......rear lights
der Sicherheitsgurt (e) . seat belt

anrufen *irreg sep* .... to phone
anspringen* *irreg* .... to start (of engine)
sich beeilen † .... to hurry
funktionieren † .... to work
kaputt gehen* *irreg* ..... to break down
eine Panne haben *irreg*.....to break down
halten *irreg* .... to stop
platzen* † .... to burst (tyre)
reparieren †.................. to fix, repair
warten † auf (+ Acc).... to wait for

WHAT TO SEE AND GETTING AROUND

Ausflüge **Outings**

der Feiertag (e) .... (public) holiday
der Freizeitpark (s) .... theme park
die Klassenfahrt (en) .... class trip
die Kirmes .... funfair
das Picknick (s) .... picnic
die Rundfahrt (en) .... guided tour (coach)
der Safaripark (s) .... safari park
die Sehenswürdigkeiten *pl* ..... sights
der Spaziergang (-gänge) ... walk
der Stadtbummel .... stroll around town
die Tour (en) .... tour
die Wanderung (en) ...... hike, long walk

Wie komme ich am besten ...? **How do I get to ...?**

Entschuldigen Sie, bitte! ... Excuse me
Gehen Sie geradeaus! ... Go straight on
Nehmen Sie die B52! ... Take the B52
Biegen Sie rechts ab! .... Turn right
Biegen Sie links ab! ..... Turn left
Gehen Sie über die Straße! ...... Cross the road
Folgen Sie den Pfeilen! .... Follow the arrows
Vielen Dank! .... Thank you very much

For **buildings** see page 68
For **landmarks** see page 68

Wo ist das? **Where is it?**

10 Kilometer (km) von..... 10 km from
500 Meter (m) entfernt..... 500 metres away
zwei Meilen entfernt .... two miles away
an der Ampel vorbei..... past the crossroads
an der Straßenecke .... on the street corner
gegenüber der Bank...... opposite the bank
hinter dem Theater .... behind the theatre
in der Nähe vom Platz...... near the square
neben der Post .... next to the post office
vor dem Kino .... outside the cinema
vor dem Kiosk............. in front of the kiosk
ganz in der Nähe........... close by
hier in der Nähe .... near here

Schilder **Signs**

Anlieger frei .... residents only
Ausstieg........................ get off here
Baustelle .... road works
bitte einordnen............. get in lane
den Rasen nicht betreten .. keep off the grass
Einbahnstraße .... one way street
Einstieg......................... get on here
Fußgängerzone .... pedestrian zone
Halteverbot .... no stopping
keine Zufahrt .... no entry
Parkverbot .... no parking
Rad fahren verboten ..... no cycling
Straße gesperrt............. road closed
Touristeninformation.... tourist information
Umleitung..................... diversion
zu den Gleisen .... to the platforms

For **shop signs** see page 40

Verkehrsmittel **Means of transport**

das Auto (s).................. car
der Bus (se).................. bus
der Dampfer (-)............ steamer, riverboat
das Fahrrad (-räder) ...... bike
das Flugzeug (e)........... plane
der Hubschrauber (-) .... helicopter
der Lastwagen (-).......... lorry
der Lieferwagen (-) .... van
der LKW (s)................. lorry
das Mofa (s) .... moped
das Motorrad (-räder).... motorbike
das Mountainbike (s) .... mountain bike
der PKW (s)................. car
der Reisebus (se) .... coach
der Roller (-)................ scooter
die S-Bahn (en) .... local train
die Straßenbahn (en) .... tram

das Taxi (s) .... taxi
die U-Bahn (en) .... underground, metro
die öffentlichen Verkehrsmittel *pl*
.... public transport
der Wagen (-) .... car
der Zug (Züge) .... train

Bahnreisen **Train travel**
die Abfahrt (en) .... departure
die Abreise (n) .... departure
die Ankunft .... arrival
die Auskunft .... information
die Bahn .... railway
die Eisenbahn (en) .... railway
die Eisenbahnlinie (n) .. railway line
der Fahrgast (-gäste) ..... passenger
der Fahrplan (-pläne) .... timetable
die Reise (n) .... journey
die Verbindung (en) ..... connection
die Verspätung (en) ...... delay
das (Reise)Ziel (e) .... destination

der D-Zug (-züge) .... express train
der Eilzug (-züge) .... regional express train
der ICE-Zug (-Züge) ..... Inter-City train
der Inter-Regio .... regional express
der Nahverkehrszug ...... local train
der Nichtraucher .... non-smoker
der Personenzug (-züge) ... slow train
die Raucherzone (e) ...... smoking area
der Schnellzug (-züge) ...... express train

die einfache Fahrkarte (n) . single ticket
die Fahrkarte (n) .... ticket
der Fahrschein (e) .... ticket
die Reservierung (en) ... reservation
die Rückfahrkarte (n) ... return ticket
der Zuschlag (Zuschläge) ...... supplement

erster Klasse .... first class
zweiter Klasse .... second class
im Voraus .... in advance

der Bahnhof (-höfe) ..... railway station
die Bahnhofshalle (n) .. station foyer
der Bahnsteig (e) .... platform
DB (Deutsche Bahn) .... German railways
der Fahrkartenschalter (-) ... ticket office
das Gepäck .... luggage
die Gepäckaufbewahrung ... left luggage
das Gepäckschließfach (-fächer)
.... left luggage locker
das Gleis (e) .... platform, track number
der Hauptbahnhof .... main station
der Taxistand .... taxi rank
der Wartesaal (-säle) .... waiting room

das Abteil (e) .... compartment
der Liegewagen (-) .... couchette car
der Schlafwagen (-) ..... sleeping car
der Speisewagen (-) ..... dining/buffet car
der Wagen (-) .... carriage

besetzt .... occupied
frei .... free, unoccupied
planmäßig .... according to timetable
pünktlich .... on time
verspätet .... late, delayed
werktags .... Monday to Saturday
wochentags .... on weekdays

abfahren* *irreg sep* ...... to leave (from)
abholen *sep* .... to meet, pick up
ankommen* *irreg sep* .. to arrive
aussteigen* *irreg sep* ... to get off/out of
einsteigen* *irreg sep* ... to get on/into
erreichen † .... to reach
mit dem Zug fahren* *irreg* .... to go by train
kontrollieren † .... to examine, check
den Zug nehmen *irreg* . to catch the train
umsteigen* *irreg sep* ... to change trains
verpassen † .... to miss (train, etc)

Bus und Straßenbahn **Bus and tram travel**

der Busbahnhof (-höfe) .... bus station
die Bushaltestelle (n).... bus stop
der Lautsprecher (-)...... loudspeaker
die Linie (n)................. line, route
die Nummer (n)........... number

der Entwerter (-)........... ticket validating machine
die Fahrkarte (n).......... ticket
der Fahrkartenautomat (en) *wk*
.... ticket machine
der Fahrpreis (e) .... fare
die Kontrolle (n).......... check (of tickets)
die Sonderfahrt (en) ..... special (charter)
die Streifenkarte (n) ..... book of tickets
die Zehnerkarte (n)....... strip of ten tickets

alle zehn Minuten......... every ten minutes
jede Stunde.................. every hour

entwerten † .... to time stamp a ticket
mit dem Bus fahren* *irreg* .... to go by bus
mit dem Reisebus fahren* ..... to go by coach

Mit dem Taxi fahren **Taking a taxi**

der Preis (e) .... taxi fare
der Taxameter.............. taxi meter
der Taxifahrer (-) .... taxi driver

abbestellen † *sep* .... to cancel
ein Taxi (online) buchen .. to book a taxi (on line)
ein Taxi rufen † .... to phone for a taxi

Country	**Meaning**	**Inhabitant**	**Inhabitant**	**Adjective**
Das Vereinigte Königsreich		**The United Kingdom**		
Großbritannien	Britain	der Brite (n)	die Britin (nen)	britisch
England	England	der Engländer (-)	die Engländerin (nen)	englisch
Nordirland	N Ireland	der Ire (n) *wk*	die Irin (nen)	irisch
Schottland	Scotland	der Schotte (n) *wk*	die Schottin (nen)	schottisch
Wales	Wales	der Waliser (-)	die Waliserin (nen)	walisisch
Deutschsprachige Länder und Nachbarländer		**German-speaking countries and neighbours**		
Deutschland	Germany	der Deutsche (n) *wk*	die Deutsche (n)	deutsch
Österreich	Austria	der Österreicher (-)	die Österreicherin (nen)	österreichisch
die Schweiz	Switzerland	der Schweizer (-)	die Schweizerin (nen)	schweizerisch
Luxemburg	Luxembourg	der Luxemburger (-)	die Luxemburgerin	luxemburgisch
Italien	Italy	der Italiener (-)	die Italienerin (nen)	italienisch
Belgien	Belgium	der Belgier (-)	die Belgierin (nen)	belgisch
Liechtenstein	Liechtenstein	der Liechtensteiner (-)	die Liechtensteinerin	liechtensteinisch
Frankreich	France	der Franzose (n) *wk*	die Französin (nen)	französisch
die Niederlande	Netherlands	der Niederländer (-)	die Niederländerin	niederländisch
Polen	Poland	der Pole (n) *wk*	die Polin (nen)	polnisch
Dänemark	Denmark	der Däne (n) *wk*	die Dänin (nen)	dänisch
die Slowakei	Slovakia	der Slowake (n) *wk*	die Slowakin (nen)	slowakisch
Tschechien	Czech Republic	der Tscheche (n) *wk*	die Tschechin (nen)	tschechisch
Ungarn	Hungary	der Ungar (en) *wk*	die Ungarin (nen)	ungarisch

Andere Länder **Other countries**

die Antillen *pl*............... West Indies
Bangladesch .... Bangladesh
die Bundesrepublik ...... Germany
China .... China
Griechenland .... Greece
Indien............................ India
Jamaika......................... Jamaica
Japan............................. Japan
Namibia .... Namibia
Pakistan .... Pakistan
Portugal .... Portugal
Russland .... Russia
Spanien .... Spain
die Türkei .... Turkey
die USA *pl*.................... USA
die Vereinigten Staaten *pl* ..... United States

amerikanisch .... American
australisch..................... Australian
bangladeschisch............ Bangladeshi
chinesisch .... Chinese
europäisch .... European
griechisch .... Greek
indisch .... Indian
jamaikanisch................. Jamaican
japanisch....................... Japanese
namibisch .... Namibian
pakistanisch.................. Pakistani
portugiesisch .... Portuguese
russisch......................... Russian
spanisch .... Spanish
türkisch......................... Turkish
westindisch................... West Indian

Regionen **Regions**

Bayern .... Bavaria
der Schwarzwald .... the Black Forest
das Rheinland .... the Rhineland

Städte **Towns**

Basel .... Basle, Basel
Brügge .... Bruges
Brüssel .... Brussels
Edinburg .... Edinburgh
Genf.............................. Geneva
Hannover .... Hanover
Köln .... Cologne
Lüttich........................... Liège
München .... Munich
Venedig......................... Venice
Wien .... Vienna

Seen, Flüsse, Berge
Lakes, seas, rivers, mountains

der Atlantik .... Atlantic
der (Ärmel)Kanal......... the English Channel
das Mittelmeer .... Mediterranean
die Nordsee.................. North Sea
die Ostsee .... Baltic Sea

die Alpen *pl* .... Alps
der Bodensee................ Lake Constance
die Donau .... the Danube
die Mosel .... the Moselle
der Rhein...................... the Rhine
die Themse .... the Thames

Kontinente **Continents**

Afrika........................... Africa
Asien............................ Asia
Australien .... Australia
Europa.......................... Europe
Nordamerika .... North America
Südamerika .... South America

HOME AND ENVIRONMENT

HOME AND LOCAL AREA

Häuser **Housing**

der Bauernhof (-höfe)... farm
der Bungalow (s).......... bungalow
das Doppelhaus (-häuser)
.... semi-detached house
die Eigentumswohnung (en)
.... owner-occupied flat
das Einfamilienhaus (-häuser)...detached house
das Gebäude (n)............ building
das Haus (Häuser) .... house
das Hochhaus (-häuser)....tower block
die Mietwohnung (en)......rented flat
das Reihenhaus (-häuser).. terraced house
die Sozialwohnung (en)
...........................housing association flat
das Studio (s)................ bedsit
der Wohnblock (s)........ block of flats
die Wohnung (en) .... flat

der Besitzer (-).............. owner
der Bewohner (-) .... resident
die Miete (n)................. rent
der Mieter (-)................ tenant
der Umzug.................... house move

Die Adresse **Address**

die Adresse (n) .... address
die E-Mail-Adresse ...... email address
die Faxnummer (n)....... fax number
die (Haus)Nummer (n)..... (house) number
die Postleitzahl (en) ..... postcode
die Telefonnummer (n).... phone number
der Wohnort (e)............ place of residence

die Allee (n) .... avenue
die Brücke (n) .... bridge
die Gasse (n) .... passage, alley
die Hauptstraße (n)....... main road
der Kai (s)..................... embankment, quay
der Platz (Plätze) ....square
die Sackgasse (n)..........cul de sac
die Straße (n) ....street, road
der Weg (e)...................lane, path, way
das Zentrum (Zentren) ..centre

ausbauen *sep*.................to extend, enlarge
beleuchten † ....to light up
sanieren † ....to do up, sort out
umziehen *irreg sep*.......to move house
wohnen ....to live, dwell

Die Gegend **Local area**

das Dorf (Dörfer) ....village
der Kreis (e)..................county; district
das Land (Länder).........region; country; state
das Meer (e) ....sea
der See (n) ....lake
die See (n) ....sea
die Stadt (Städte)..........town
das Viertel (-)................district of town
der Vorort (e)................suburb

auf dem Land................in the country
in der Stadt ....in the town
im Norden.....................in the north
im Osten ....in the east
im Süden.......................in the south
im Westen.....................in the west

nördlich von (+ Dat).....north of
östlich von (+ Dat) ....east of
südlich von (+ Dat).......south of
westlich von (+ Dat).....west of

Allgemeines **General**

der Aufzug (-züge) ....lift
der Eingang (-gänge) ....entrance
der Fahrstuhl (-stühle) ..lift

der Feuerlöscher (-) ...... fire extinguisher
der Flur (e) .... hall
der Gang (Gänge) .... corridor
die (Haus)Tür (e) .... (front) door
der Lift (s) .... lift
der Plan (Pläne) .... plan
der Stock (-) .... floor, storey
die Stufe (n) .... step
die Treppe (n) .... staircase
der Treppenflur (e) .... landing

im Erdgeschoss .... on the ground floor
im Keller .... in the cellar
im ersten Stock .... on the first floor
oben .... upstairs
unten .... downstairs

Die Zimmer **Rooms**
der Abstellraum (-räume) ... store room
das Arbeitszimmer (-) ... study
das Badezimmer (-) ...... bathroom
der Dachboden (-böden) ... attic, loft
die Diele (n) .... hall
das Esszimmer (-) .... dining room
die Garage (n) .... garage
der Hausflur (e) .... hall
der Keller (-) .... cellar, basement
das Kinderzimmer (-) ... playroom
das Klo (s) .... toilet, loo
die Küche (n) .... kitchen
das Schlafzimmer (-) .... bedroom
der Speicher (-) .... attic, loft
die Toilette (n) .... toilet
die Waschküche (n) ...... utility room
der Wintergarten (-gärten) ..... conservatory
das Wohnzimmer (-) ..... living-room, lounge

Das Schlafzimmer **Bedroom**
das Bett (en) .... bed
das Buch (Bücher) .... book
die Gardine (n) .... net curtain
die Haarbürste (n) .... hairbrush
der Kamm (Kämme) ..... comb

der Kasten (-) .... box
die Kiste (n) .... chest, box
der Kleiderschrank (-schränke) .... wardrobe
die Kommode (n) .... chest of drawers
die Lampe (n) .... lamp
der Nachttisch (e) .... bedside table
das Poster (-) .... poster
das Regal (e) .... shelf, shelving
der Schreibtisch (e) ...... desk
die Schublade (n) .... drawer
der Spiegel (-) .... mirror
der Teppich (e) .... rug
der Vorhang (-hänge) ... curtain
der Wecker (-) .... alarm clock
eigen .... own, private

die CD (s) .... CD
der Computer (-) .... computer
der Fernseher (-) .... TV set
der Föhn (e) .... hairdryer
der MP3-Player (-) .... MP3 Player
der Radiowecker (-) ..... radio alarm
das Spielzeug *no pl* ...... toys
die Stereoanlage (n) ..... stereo system
das Videospiel (e) .... video game

Die Küche **Kitchen**
der Elektroherd (e) .... electric cooker
die Essecke (n) .... dining space
der Gasherd (e) .... gas cooker
der Kühlschrank (-schränke) .... fridge
der Mikrowellenherd (e) ... microwave (oven)
der (Back)Ofen (Öfen) ...... oven
die Spülmaschine (n) ... dishwasher
die Tiefkühltruhe (n) ... freezer
die Waschmaschine (n) ..... washing machine
tiefgefroren .... deep frozen

das Bügeleisen (-) .... iron
der Schrank (Schränke) ..... cupboard
das Spülbecken (-) .... sink
der Staubsauger (-) .... vacuum cleaner

der Toaster (-)............... toaster
die Trockenschleuder (n) .. spin dryer
der Wäschetrockner (-)...... tumble dryer

der Abfalleimer (-) .... rubbish bin
die Bratpfanne (n) .... frying pan
das Bügelbrett (er) .... ironing board
der Dosenöffner (-)....... can opener
der Flaschenöffner (-)... bottle opener
das Geschirrtuch (-tücher)...tea towel
die Streichhölzer *pl* ...... matches
das Tablett (s) .... tray
das Telefon (e).............. telephone
der Topf (Töpfe)........... saucepan
das Waschpulver .... washing powder

Das Esszimmer **Dining room**
die Anrichte (n)............ sideboard
das Gemälde (-) .... painting (picture)
die Kerze (n) .... candle
der Stuhl (Stühle) .... chair
der Tisch (e) .... table
die Tischdecke (n)........ tablecloth
das Tischtuch (-tücher)..... tablecloth

Das Wohnzimmer **Living room, Lounge**
das Bücherregal (e)....... book-case
der CD-Spieler (-) .... CD player
der Couchtisch (e) .... coffee table
der DVD-Spieler (-) ..... DVD player
der Fernseher (-) .... TV set
das Foto (s) .... photo
der Holzboden (-böden) ... wooden floor
der Kamin (e) .... fireplace
das Kissen (-)................ cushion
das Klavier (e) .... piano
der Lehnstuhl (-stühle) ..... armchair
der Sessel (-)................ armchair
das Sofa (s) .... sofa, settee
die Stehlampe (n) .... standard lamp
die Stereoanlage (n) ..... stereo system
der Teppichboden (-böden)....fitted carpet
die Uhr (en) .... clock
die Vase (n) .... vase

hängen *irreg* .... to hang
heizen † .... to heat

Das Badezimmer **Bathroom**
das Bad .... bath (activity)
das Badetuch (-tücher).. bath towel
die Badewanne (n)........ bath (tub)
das Bidet (s) .... bidet
das Deo (s) .... deodorant
die Dusche (n) .... shower
das Handtuch (-tücher) ..... towel
der Rasierapparat (e)..... razor
das Schaumbad .... bubble bath
der Schwamm (Schwämme).. sponge
die Seife........................ soap
das Shampoo (s)............ shampoo
der Spiegel (-) .... mirror
das Toilettenpapier .... toilet paper
das Waschbecken (-)..... wash basin
der Waschlappen (-) ..... flannel
der Wasserhahn (-hähne).. tap
die Zahnbürste (n) .... toothbrush
die Zahnpasta .... toothpaste
heißes Wasser.............. hot water
kaltes Wasser................ cold water

For **helping at home** see page 67
For **daily routine** see page 67

Allgemeines **General**
der Anstrich .... paint
die Aussicht (en) .... view
der Balkon (s) .... balcony
das Dach (Dächer) .... roof
die Decke (n) .... ceiling
der Dekor .... décor
das Fenster (-) .... window
der Fußboden (-böden) ..... floor
die Gartenpforte (n)...... gate
das Glas........................ glass
der Griff (e) .... handle
die Klingel (n) .... doorbell
die Mauer (n)................ wall (external)

die Möbel *pl* ....furniture
der Quadratmeter (-) (m^2)......square metre
der Rollladen (-läden)...(roller) shutter
das Schloss (Schlösser).... lock
der Schornstein (e) ....chimney
die Tapete (n) ....wallpaper
die Wand (Wände) ....wall (internal)

das Gas.........................gas
die Glühbirne (n)..........light bulb
der Heizkörper (-).........radiator
das Kabel (-) ....flex
das Licht (er)................light
das Putzen.....................cleaning
der Schalter (-).............switch
die Steckdose (n)..........electric socket
der Stecker (-)..............plug
der Strom ....electricity, current
die (Zentral)Heizung ....(central) heating

Die Garage **Garage**
das Auto (s)... ....car
das Fahrrad (-räder) ......bike
das Motorrad (-räder)....motorbike
der Rasenmäher (-).......lawnmower
der Roller (-)................scooter
der Wagen (-)...............car
das Werkzeug *no pl* ......tools

Der Garten **Garden**
der Apfelbaum (-bäume) .. apple tree
der Baum (Bäume) ....tree
die Blume (n) ....flower
das Blumenbeet (e).......flower bed
der Busch (Büsche) ......bush
das Gemüse..................vegetable
der Gemüsegarten (-gärten)
...............................vegetable garden
die Gemüsesorte (n) .... type of vegetable
das Gewächshaus (-häuser) ... greenhouse
das Gras ....grass
die Hecke (n)................hedge
das Obst ....fruit
der Obstbaum (-bäume).....fruit tree
die Obstsorte (n) .... type of fruit
die Pflanze (n) .... plant
der Rasen (-) .... lawn
die Rose (n) .... rose
der Schuppen (-) .... shed
der Sonnenschirm (e)... parasol, sunshade
die Tanne (n) .... fir tree
die Terrasse (n)........... patio, terrace
der Zaun (Zäune) .... fence

Wie ist das Haus? **What is it like?**
bequem .... comfortable
elegant......................... elegant
eng .... cramped
freundlich.................... welcoming
gemütlich .... cosy
geräumig .... roomy
hübsch......................... pretty
leer .... empty
luxuriös .... luxurious
möbliert .... furnished
nagelneu...................... brand new
notwendig .... necessary
perfekt......................... perfect
praktisch .... practical
schick .... smart
seltsam .... odd, strange
typisch......................... typical
unentbehrlich .... essential
vornehm...................... posh

in gutem Zustand ....in good condition
in schlechtem Zustand ...... in poor condition

Wo ist es? **Where is it?**
im Erdgeschoss........... on the ground floor
im ersten Stock .... on the first floor
oben/unten .... upstairs/downstairs
hinter dem Haus.......... behind the house
vor dem Haus.............. in front of the house
mit Gartenblick........... with a garden view
mit Straßenblick .... with a street view

Die Tagesroutine **Daily Routine**

in der Schule ankommen* *irreg sep* .... to arrive at school
sich anziehen *irreg sep*..... to get dressed
aufstehen* *irreg sep*..... to get up
aufwachen* *sep*........... to wake up
sich ausziehen *irreg sep*.... to get undressed
sich duschen................ to shower
zu Abend essen *irreg*... to have evening meal
zu Mittag essen *irreg*... to have lunch
frühstücken.................. to have breakfast
ins Bett gehen* *irreg*.... to go to bed
Hausaufgaben machen...... to do homework
das Haus verlassen *irreg*... to leave the house
sich waschen *irreg*....... to get washed

ausschlafen *irreg sep*.... to have a lie in
sich beeilen †............... to rush
sich die Haare bürsten † .... to brush one's hair
einschlafen* *irreg sep*.. to fall asleep
in die Stadt gehen* *irreg*... to go into town
sich hinlegen *sep*.......... to lie down
sich kämmen................ to comb one's hair
sich die Zähne putzen †.... to clean one's teeth
sich rasieren †............. to shave
sich schminken............. to put on make-up
sich schmücken............ to put on jewellery
auf sein* *irreg*............. to be up
Sport treiben *irreg*........ to do sport
sich die Haare trocknen †... to dry one's hair
sich umziehen *irreg sep*.... to get changed
wecken......................... to wake s.o

Die Mahlzeiten **Meals**

das Abendessen (-)....... dinner, evening meal
das Frühstück (e).......... breakfast
der Imbiss (-e)............. snack
Kaffee und Kuchen....... afternoon coffee and cake
das Mittagessen (-)........ lunch, midday meal
das Picknick (s)............ picnic

For **foods** see page 17
For **times** see page 8
For **days of the week** see page 8

Im Haushalt helfen **Helping at home**

den Tisch abräumen *sep*.... to clear the table
abspülen *sep*................ to wash up
abtrocknen † *sep*........... to dry dishes
abwaschen *irreg sep*..... to wash up
im Garten arbeiten †..... to work in the garden
auf Kinder aufpassen † *sep*.... to baby sit
mein Zimmer aufräumen *sep* .... to tidy my room
die Spülmaschine ausräumen *sep* .... to empty the dishwasher
bügeln........................... to iron
den Tisch decken.......... to set the table
die Katze füttern........... to feed the cat
mit dem Hund Gassi gehen* *irreg* .... to walk the dog
Blumen gießen *irreg*..... to water the flowers
kehren........................... to sweep
kochen.......................... to cook
mein Bett machen......... to make my bed
Einkäufe machen.......... to do shopping
Hausarbeit machen....... to do housework
den Rasen mähen.......... to mow the lawn
putzen †........................ to clean
Staub saugen................. to vacuum
spülen........................... to wash up
das Auto waschen *irreg* .... to wash the car
Staub wischen.............. to dust

HOME TOWN, NEIGHBOURHOOD AND REGION

In der Stadt **In town**

Gebäude **Buildings**

der Bahnhof (-höfe)......station
die Bank (en)................bank
die Bibliothek (en) ....library
das Büro (s)...................office
das Einkaufszentrum (-zentren) ....shopping centre
die Fabrik (en)..............factory
das Geschäft (e) ....shop
der Jugendklub (s)........youth club
das Kino (s)...................cinema
die Kirche (n) ....church
das Krankenhaus (-häuser) .... hospital
der Laden (Läden) ....shop
der Markt (Märkte).......market
der Park (s) ....park
das Parkhaus (-häuser) ....multi-storey car park
der Parkplatz (-plätze)..car park
die Post.........................post office
das Postamt (-ämter).....post office
das Rathaus (-häuser)....town hall
die Schule (-n) ....school
das Schwimmbad (-bäder).. swimming pool
die Sparkasse (n) ....bank
der Spielplatz (-plätze)..... playground
die Tankstelle (n) ....petrol station

die Burg (en) ....castle (fortified)
der Campingplatz (-plätze).... campsite
der Dom (e) ....cathedral
das Hotel (s)..................hotel
das Informationsbüro (s)........ tourist office
die Kathedrale (n).........cathedral
die Kunstgalerie (n)......art gallery
das Museum (Museen) ......museum
das Schloss (Schlösser).......... stately home
das Stadion (Stadien)....stadium
das Theater (-)..............theatre
der Turm (Türme)........ tower
das Verkehrsamt (-ämter) ..tourist office

das Altenheim (e)......... old people's home
die Altstadt .... town centre
der Busbahnhof (-höfe)......bus station
die Eisbahn (en).......... ice rink
der Flughafen (-häfen). airport
die Innenstadt .... town centre
die Jugendherberge (n) .....youth hostel
die Klinik (en) .... clinic, hospital
das Polizeirevier (e) ..... police station
die Polizeiwache (n) .... police station
das Reisebüro (s).......... travel agency
das Sportzentrum (-zentren)... sports centre
die Stadtmitte (n)......... town centre
die Telefonzelle (n) ..... phone box
der Wohnblock (s) .... block of flats
der Zeitungskiosk (e) ... newspaper stand

Orientierungspunkte **Landmarks**

die Allee (n)................ avenue (with trees)
die Ampel .... traffic lights, pelican crossing
die Autobahn (en)........ motorway
der Briefkasten (-kästen).......letter box
die Brücke (n)............. bridge
die Bushaltestelle (n)... bus stop
die Ecke (n) .... corner
die Kreuzung (en)........ crossroads
das Kunstwerk (e) .... work of art
der Marktplatz (-plätze)....market square
der Palast (Paläste)....... palace
der Platz (Plätze).......... square
die Statue (n) .... statue
die Straßenecke (n)...... street corner
die U-Bahn .... underground

der Bahnübergang (-gänge) ..level crossing
die Baustelle (n).......... roadworks
der Bürgersteig (e) .... pavement

das Denkmal (-mäler)...monument
die Fußgängerzone (n) ..... pedestrian zone
der Hafen (Häfen) ....port
die Unterführung (en) .. subway
der Verkehr...................traffic
der Verkehrskreisel ......roundabout
der Zebrastreifen (-) .....pedestrian crossing

der Fussweg (e) ....footpath
die Graffiti *pl* ....graffiti
die Grünanlage (n) ....green space
der Kirchturm (-türme)..... church tower
der Radweg (e) ....cycle route
der Stadtteil (e)............part of a town
das Straßenschild (er)...road sign
die Umgehungsstraße (n)... ring road, bypass

Im Park **In the park**
die Bank (Bänke) ....bench
die Blume (n) ....flower
das Blumenbeet (e).......flower bed
der Brunnen (-)............fountain
der Kinderspielplatz (-plätze)..... play area
die Schaukel (n) ....swing
die Wiese (n)................grassed area

Leute **People**
der Autofahrer (-).........motorist
der Fußgänger (-)..........pedestrian
die Menge (n)...............crowd
der Polizist (en) *wk*.......policeman
die Polizistin (nen).......policewoman
der Radfahrer (-)...........cyclist
der Stadtbewohner (-)...city dweller

Auf dem Land **In the country**
der Acker (Äcker) ....field
der Baum (Bäume).......tree
das Feld (er)..................field (arable)
das Ferienhaus (-häuser)... holiday cottage
der Fluss (Flüsse) ....river
das Gras ....grass
die Hecke (n)................hedge
der Hof (Höfe).............yard
der Hügel (-) ....hill
die Kapelle (n).............chapel
das Land........................countryside
die Landschaft (en).......countryside, scenery
die Natur.......................nature
das Ufer (-)....................riverbank
der Wald (Wälder)........forest, wood
der Wanderweg (e) ....footpath
die Wiese (n) ....pasture, meadow

Auf dem Bauernhof **On the farm**
der Bauer (n) *wk* ....farmer
die Bäuerin (nen)..........female farmer
das Bauernhaus (-häuser).... farmhouse
die Ernte (n)..................harvest
die Hühner *pl*................hens
die Kuh (Kühe).............cow
der Landwirt (en).........farmer
das Schaf (e) ....sheep
das Schwein (e)............pig
der Stall (Ställe)...........stable
der Traktor (en) ....tractor
der Weinbauer (n) *wk* ...wine grower
der Weinberg (-e) ....vineyard
der Weingarten (-gärten) .. vineyard

Die Haustiere **Pets**
der Goldfisch (e)..........goldfish
der Hamster (-) ....hamster
der Hase (n) *wk*............rabbit, hare
der Hund (e).................dog
die Hündin (nen) ....female dog
der Käfig (e) ....cage
der Kanarienvogel (-vögel)... canary
das Kaninchen (-)..........rabbit
der Kater (-) ....tom-cat
das Kätzchen (-)............kitten
die Katze (n) ....cat
die Maus (Mäuse).........mouse
das Meerschweinchen (-).... guinea pig
der Papagei (en)............parrot

das Pferd (e)..................horse
die Schildkröte (n)........tortoise
das Tier (e)....................animal
das Tierheim (e)............animal refuge
der Vogel (Vögel).........bird
der Wellensittich (e).....budgerigar
der Welpe (n) *wk*..........puppy
die Wüstenspringmaus (-mäuse).... gerbil

dressieren †...................to train
füttern ....to feed
ein Tier halten *irreg* .....to keep an animal
pfeifen *irreg* ....to whistle

Wie ist es? What is it like?
anonym ....anoymous
benachbart ....nearby, neighbouring
dünn bevölkert.............sparsely populated
breit ....wide
ehemalig ....ex-, former
entzückend...................charming
flach ....flat
fremd ....foreign, unfamiliar
gefährlich......................dangerous
historisch ....historic
hügelig..........................hilly
industriell ....industrial
malerisch ....picturesque
mehrere.........................several
nah ....near, nearby
in der Nähe ....near, nearby
natürlich........................natural
öffentlich ....public
örtlich ....local
steil ....steep
still.................................peaceful
tief ....deep
touristisch ....touristy
überbevölkert................overpopulated
verschmutzt ....polluted
wild...............................wild

umgeben von (+ Dat) ...surrounded by

Vergleiche mit anderen Wohnorten
Comparisons with other areas
das Einkaufszentrum (-zentren)
.... shopping centre
das Kaufhaus (-häuser) .....department store
das Sportzentrum (-zentren)... sports centre
öffentliche Verkehrsmittel *pl*
.... public transport
viel Verkehr .... a lot of traffic
viel zu tun .... lots to do
nichts zu tun................ nothing to do

sowohl … als (auch).... as well as
so groß wie .... as big as
so klein wie................. as small as
fürchterlich .... awful
langweilig .... boring
sehr interessant .... very interesting
nicht so interessant ...... less interesting
nicht so industriell .... less industrial
größer (als).................. bigger (than)
kleiner (als)................. smaller (than)

For **names of buildings** see page 68
For **free time activities** see page 30
For **local area** see page 63
For **going into town** etc see page 36

Umgebung Geography
der Bach (Bäche) .... stream
der Berg (e)................. mountain
die Entfernung (en)...... distance
der Fels (en) .... cliff, rock face
das Festland................. mainland (not island)
der Fluss (Flüsse)......... river
das Gebiet (e) .... region
das Gebirge (-) .... mountain range
der Gipfel (-)............... summit
die Halbinsel................ peninsular
die Höhe (n)................ height
die Höhle (n)............... cave
der Hügel (-) .... hill
die Insel (n)................. island

das Klima (s) .... climate
die Klippe (n) .... (seaside) cliff
die Küste (n)................. coast
die Lage (n) .... situation, position
das Land .... countryside
das Land (Länder)......... country, state
die Länge...................... length
der Mond (e)................. the moon
der See (n) .... lake
die See (n) .... sea
die Sonne....................... the sun
der Stern (e).................. star (in sky)
das Tal (Täler) .... valley
die Tiefe .... depth

das Dorf (Dörfer).......... village
die Grenze (n) .... border
die Großstadt (-städte)...... city
die Hauptstadt (-städte).... capital
die Industrie (n)............ industry
das Industriegebiet (e) .. industrial area
die Industriestadt (-städte)..... industrial town
die Landwirtschaft .... agriculture

der Lärm .... noise
die Provinz (en)............ province
die Stadt (Städte).......... town
der Vorort (e)................ suburb

das Inland...................... home (not abroad)
das Ausland.................. abroad

mitten in .... in the middle of

Nützliche Verben **Useful verbs**
sich befinden *irreg* .... to be situated
fließen* *irreg*................ to flow
bis … gehen* *irreg*....... to go as far as
überqueren *insep* .... to cross
an (+ Dat) vorbeigehen* *irreg sep*
.... to go past
weiterfahren* *irreg sep*
.... to drive on, continue
weitergehen* *irreg sep*
.... to walk on, continue

THE ENVIRONMENT AND ITS PROBLEMS

Allgemeines **General**
die Atembeschwerden *pl*
.... breathing difficulties
die Auswirkung (en) .... effect
der Effekt (e) .... effect
die Erde .... earth (planet; soil)
die Folge (n)................. consequence
der ökologische Fußabdruck
.... carbon footprint
der Grund (Gründe)...... reason
der Kontinent (e) .... continent
die Luftverschmutzung .... air pollution
die Natur .... nature
der Nordpol .... north pole
das Ökosystem (e) .... ecosystem

der Planet (en) *wk*......... planet
das Polareis................... polar ice cap
der Sauerstoff .... oxygen
das Schmelzen .... thawing
der Schnee .... snow
das Schwefeldioxid....... sulphur dioxide
der Südpol .... south pole
die wissenschaftlichen Tatsachen *pl*
.... the scientific facts
die Umwelt................... environment
der Urwald.................... rainforest
die Welt (en)................. world
die Wüste (n)................ wilderness, desert
die Zukunft................... future
die Zunahme (n) .... increase

chemisch......................chemical
emotional.....................emotive
extrem..........................extreme
fürchterlich ....terrible, appalling
international.................international
Kern- ....nuclear
ökologisch, Öko- ....ecological
rücksichtslos.................irresponsible
schädlich......................harmful
umweltfeindlich....environmentally damaging
umweltfreundlich ....environmentally friendly
unwiderruflich ....irreversible
verantwortlich (für)......responsible (for)
wirtschaftlich...............economical, economic
ohne Zweifel................without a doubt

abnehmen *irreg sep*......to fall (temperature)
anbauen *sep* ....to grow, cultivate
ändern..........................to change, modify
aufheizen † *sep*............to heat up
bedrohen †....................to threaten
beenden † ....to put a stop to
beschädigen †...............to damage
brennen *irreg*................to burn, parch
drohen (+ Dat).............to threaten
einatmen † *sep*.............to breathe in
eindringen* *irreg sep* ...to invade
entsorgen † ....to dispose of
erschöpfen † ....to exhaust
filtern ....to filter
leeren ....to empty
pflücken.......................to pick
reduzieren †..................to reduce
sinken* *irreg* ....to fall (temperature)
spenden †......................to donate
steigen* *irreg* ....to rise (temperature)
überschwemmen *insep* ..... to flood
verbieten *irreg*..............to forbid
sich verbreiten † ....to spread
verderben †...................to spoil
vergiften † ....to poison
verhindern † ....to prevent
vermindern †............... to decrease
verpesten †.................. to pollute
verschmutzen †........... to pollute
versuchen †................. to try
verteidigen † .... to defend
wagen.......................... to dare
zunehmen *irreg sep* ..... to increase

Umweltverschmutzer Sources of pollution

die Abgase *pl*.............. exhaust gases
die Auspuffgase *pl*....... car exhaust gases
der Brennstoff (e)......... fuel
das Düngemittel (-)...... fertiliser
die Fabrik (en) .... factory
FCKWs....................... CFCs
der Flugverkehr........... aviation, flying
die chemischen Industrien
.... chemical industries
das Kernkraftwerk (e).. nuclear power station
die Klimaanlage (e) ..... air conditioning
die Kohle (n)............... coal
das Kraftwerk (e) .... power station
die Müllentsorgung...... waste disposal
das Pestizid (e)............ pesticide
der Schiffsverkehr........ maritime transport
die Sprühdose (n)......... aerosol
das Treibhausgas (e) .... greenhouse gas
die Umweltverschmutzung.... pollution
die Ursache (n) .... cause
der Verkehr................. traffic
der Zuwachs................ increase

Katastrophen Disasters

Aids .... AIDS
die Armut.................... poverty
die Dürre (n) .... drought
die Epidemie (n) .... epidemic
das Erdbeben (-).......... earthquake
der Hunger .... hunger
die Hungersnot (-nöte). famine
die Krankheiten *pl* .... diseases
die Lawine (n)............. avalanche

die Überschwemmung (en) ... flood
das Waldsterben .... forest dying

die Abholzung (en) ...... deforestation
das Klima .... climate
die Klimaänderung .... climate change
die Krise (n) .... crisis
der Lebensstandard .... standard of living
das Ozonloch .... hole in ozone layer
die Ozonschicht .... ozone layer
das Risiko (Risiken) ..... risk
der Treibhauseffekt ...... greenhouse effect
die Untersuchung (en) .. enquiry
die Zerstörung .... destruction

der Brand (Brände) .... fire (accidental)
die globale Erwärmung .... global warming
das (Öl)Leck (e) .... (crude oil) leak
die Ölraffinerie (n) .... oil refinery
der Öltanker (-) .... oil tanker
der Ölteppich (e) .... oil slick
der saure Regen .... acid rain
die Stadtverschmutzung ... urban pollution

Beinflussung durch Menschenhand Human intervention

die Armee .... army
die Diktatur (en) .... dictatorship
der Frieden .... peace
der Krieg (e) .... war
die Not .... need
der Streik (s) .... strike
die Vergangenheit .... the past

die Dritte Welt .... Third World
das Gesetz (e) .... law
die Monarchie (n) .... monarchy
die Politik *no pl* .... politics, policy
die Regierung (en) .... regime, government
die Republik (en) .... republic
die Wahl (en) .... election

die Bedürftigen *pl* .... the needy
die Einwanderer *pl* .... immigants
die Einwanderung .... immigration
der Mensch (en) *wk* ...... human being

der König (e) .... king
die Königin (nen) .... queen
der Minister (-) .... minister
der Präsident (en) *wk* .... President
der Premierminister (-) ..... Prime Minister
die Queen .... Elizabeth II
der Streikende ‡ .... striker
das Volk (Völker) .... the people

die Demonstration (en) ..... demonstration
die Freiheit (en) .... freedom
das Rote Kreuz .... Red Cross
die Menschenrechte *pl* ...... human rights
die Moralität .... morality
die karitativen Organisationen *pl* ... charities

bedürftig .... in need of
rechtzeitig .... in (good) time
schlaflos .... sleepless
unvorstellbar .... unimaginable

Umweltschutz Conservation

der Baum (Bäume) .... tree
das Insektizid (e) .... insecticide
das Kompostieren .... composting green waste
der ökologischer Landbau .... organic farming
die Nahrungskette .... food chain
das Pestizid (e) .... pesticide
die Rettung .... salvation
die biologische Schädlingsbekämpfung .... biological pest control
das Umweltamt .... environment agency
das Unkrautvernichtungsmittel (-) .... weed-killer
der Wald (Wälder) .... wood, forest

die Batterie (n)............. battery
die Elektrizität.............. electricity
das Elektro-Fahrzeug (e) .. electric vehicle
die Energie .... energy
die Solarenergie............ solar energy
die Solarzelle (n) .... solar panel
der (mäßige) Verbrauch
.... (moderate) consumption
die Windturbine (n)...... wind turbine

(wieder)aufladbar .... rechargeable

Vom Aussterben bedrohte Arten **Endangered species**

die Fauna .... wildlife, fauna
die Flora .... plants, flora
das Futter .... fodder
der Lebensraum .... habitat
der Regenwald.............. rain forest
die Wildblume (n) .... wild flower

die Bienen *pl* .... bees
der Frosch (Frösche)..... frog
der Igel (-)..................... hedgehog
der Kabeljau (s) .... cod
die Kröte (n)................. toad
der Marienkäfer (-) .... ladybird
der Schmetterling (e).... butterfly
der Singvogel (vögel)... songbird
der Wassermolch (e)..... newt

der Blauwal (e) .... blue whale
der Delphin (e) .... dolphin
der Eisbär (en) *wk*......... polar bear
der Elefant (en) *wk* .... elephant
das Elfenbein .... ivory
das Fell.......................... fur
der Krill .... krill
der Orang-Utan (s)........ orang-utan
der Panda (s)................. giant panda
der Stoßzahn (-zähne)... tusk
der Tiger (-) .... tiger

Wilde Tiere **Wild animals**

der Affe (n) *wk*............ monkey
das Kamel (e) .... camel
der Löwe (n) *wk*........... lion
die Schlange (n)........... snake

Adjektive **Adjectives**

Bio- .... organic
in Gefahr .... in danger
gefährdet .... in danger
global .... world, global
rar .... rare
scheu .... shy
selten .... rare
überbevölkert .... overpopulated
überstrapaziert .... overburdened
verletzt .... injured, wounded

Nützliche Verben **Useful verbs**

atmen † .... to breathe
jagen .... to hunt
kämpfen .... to fight, struggle
leben .... to live
leiden *irreg* .... to suffer
passieren* † .... to occur
schießen *irreg* .... to shoot
schützen † .... to conserve, protect
sichern .... to safeguard
sterben* *irreg* .... to die
retten † .... to save
töten † .... to kill
warnen .... to warn
wildern......................... to poach (game)

For **countryside** see page 69
For **opinions** see page 10
For **home** see page 63
For **transport** see page 59

BEING ENVIRONMENTALLY FRIENDLY

Die Umwelt verbessern
Improving the environment

der Altglascontainer (-) ..... bottle bank
das Altpapier .... recycled paper
der Brennstoff (e) .... fossil fuel
die Energieeinsparung...... saving of energy
die Energiesparlampe (n)
.... low energy light bulbs
der Flaschencontainer (-).... bottle bank
der ökologische Fußabdruck
.... carbon footprint
der Komposthaufen (-) ..... compost heap
das Recycling................ recycling
der Tourismus .... tourism
die Umwelt.................. environment
grüne Verkehrslösungen
.... green travel options
öffentliche Verkehrsmittel *pl*
.... public transport

mehr .... more
weniger......................... less
umweltfreundlich .... environmentally friendly

aufgeben *irreg sep*........ to give up
benutzen † .... to use
filtern............................ to filter
den Schaden in Grenzen halten *irreg*
.... to limit the damage
sich um die Umwelt kümmern
........to do something to save the planet
recyceln † .... to recycle
sparen .... to save
verbrauchen †.............. to consume
verwenden † .... to use
wählen .... to choose; to vote
wegwerfen *irreg sep*..... to throw away
wiederverwerten † *insep* .. to recycle

Haushaltsmüll **Domestic waste**

der Abfall...................... rubbish
die Aludose (n)............. aluminium can
die Batterie (n)............. battery
der Biomüll................... organic waste
die Einwegflasche (n)... non-returnable bottle
das Glas (Gläser) .... glass
die Klarsichtfolie .... cling film
der Kunststoff (e).......... plastic
das Metall (e) .... metal
das Mindesthaltbarkeitsdatum (-daten)
.... use by date
die Mülltonne (n).......... dustbin
das Papier...................... paper
das Pfand....................... deposit (on bottle)
die Pfandflasche (n)...... returnable bottle
die Plastiktüte (n) .... plastic bag
die Ratte (n).................. rat
die Stahldose (n)........... steel can
die Überreste *pl* .... leftovers
das Verfallsdatum (-daten) ... use by date
die Verpackung (en) ..... packaging
die Wiederverwertung ...... recycling

braun............................ brown
chemisch....................... chemical
giftig .... poisonous
grün.............................. green
klar............................... clear
Öko-.............................. ecological
vergiftet .... poisoned
wiederverwendbar .... re-usable
wirtschaftlich .... economical

produzieren † .... to produce
Müll sortieren † .... to sort rubbish
verpacken † .... to package
verschwenden † .... to waste
zerstören † .... to destroy

SPECIAL OCCASIONS IN THE HOME AND FAMILY

Glückwünsche **Best wishes**

Herzlichen Glückwunsch! .... Best Wishes!
Herzlichen Glückwunsch zum Geburtstag! .... Happy Birthday!
Hals- und Beinbruch! ... Good luck!
Ein glückliches neues Jahr! .... Happy New Year!
Frohe Ostern! .... Happy Easter!
Einen schönen Tag noch! ... Have a nice day!
Fröhliche Weihnachten! ..... Happy Christmas!
Ich gratuliere! .... Congratulations!
Viel Spaß! .... Have a good time!

Festtage **Festivals**

Chanukka...................... Chanukah
Diwali........................... Divali
Id .... Eid
das jüdische Neujahr..... Rosh Hashana
das Passah..................... Passover
Ramadan....................... Ramadan
der Sabbat.................... Sabbath

der Karneval .... Carnival
der Rosenmontag.......... day before Shrove Tuesday
der Faschingsdienstag... Shrove Tuesday
der Karfreitag .... Good Friday
Ostersonntag................. Easter Day
der erste Mai................. May 1st
der Muttertag................ Mother's Day
Pfingsten....................... Whitsun
Allerheiligen................. All Saints (Nov 1st)
der fünfte November .... Guy Fawkes Night
Weihnachten................. Christmas
der Heiligabend .... Christmas Eve
der erste Weihnachtstag..... Christmas Day
der zweite Weihnachtstag.. Boxing Day
Silvester........................ New Year's Eve
das Neujahr................... New Year's Day
Heilige Drei Könige ..... Twelfth Night

For **opinions** see page 10

Allgemeines **General**

der Ball (Bälle) .... ball, dance
der Feiertag (e)............. public holiday
das Feuerwerk *no pl*..... fireworks
die Geburtstagsparty (s).... birthday party
das Geschenk (e).......... present
die Karte (n)................. card
das Osterei (er)............. Easter egg
die Party (s).................. party
die Prozession (en) ...... religious procession
die Überraschung (en) . surprise
der Umzug (-züge)....... procession
der Weihnachtsbaum ... Christmas tree
der Weihnachtsmann ... Father Christmas
der Wunsch (Wünsche) .... wish, desire

aufgeregt .... excited
Familien- .... of the family
religiös .... religious

sich gut amüsieren † .... to have a good time
Freunde besuchen † ..... to visit friends
beten † .... to pray
Freunde einladen *irreg sep* .... to have friends round
feiern............................ to celebrate
essen gehen* *irreg*....... to go to a restaurant
organisieren † .... to organise
schenken .... to give a present
tanzen †........................ to dance

Leute **People**

der Christ (en) *wk* .... Christian
die Christin (nen)......... Christian
der Gott .... God
der/die Hindu (s).......... Hindu
der Jude (n) *wk*............ Jew
die Jüdin (nen) .... Jewess
der Muslim (e) .... Muslim
die Muslima (s)............ Muslim
der/die Sikh (s) .... Sikh

WORK AND EDUCATION

SCHOOL/COLLEGE AND FUTURE PLANS

Der Schulbesuch **School attendance**

die Schule (n) .... school
die Stufe (n) .... (key) stage
die Ganztagsschule (n)..... all-day school
der Kindergarten (-gärten)..... nursery school
die Grundschule (n)...... primary school
die private Grundschule (n) .. prep school
die Gesamtschule (n).... comprehensive school
das Gymnasium (Gymnasien) .... grammar school
die Realschule (n) .... technical secondary school
die Hauptschule (n)...... secondary modern
das Oberstufenkolleg (-kollegien) .... sixth form/tertiary college
das Internat (e)............. boarding school
die Privatschule (n) ...... public school
die Berufsschule........... Technical College
die Fachhochschule (n) .... technical university
die Universität (en) ...... university

in der 6. Klasse............. in Year 7
in der 7. Klasse............. in Year 8
in der 8. Klasse............. in Year 9
in der 9. Klasse............. in Year 10
in der 10. Klasse........... in Year 11
in der 11. Klasse........... in Year 12
in der 12. Klasse........... in Year 13
in der Oberstufe............ in the Sixth Form

Leute **People**

der Abiturient (en) *wk* .. sixth former
die Abiturientin (nen)... sixth former
der Internatsschüler (-) .... boarder
der Klassenkamerad (en) *wk* ..classmate
die Klassenkameradin (nen)...classmate
der Klassensprecher (-) ..class spokesperson
der Schüler (-) .... school student
die Schülerin (nen) ....school student
der Schulfreund (e).......school friend
die Schulfreundin (nen).....school friend
der Tagesschüler (-)......day-pupil

der Berufsberater (-) .....careers officer
der Direktor (en)...........headteacher (male)
die Direktorin (nen)......headteacher (female)
der Hausmeister (-).......caretaker
der Inspektor (en) ....inspector
der Lehrer (-) ....teacher
die Lehrerin (nen).........teacher
die Lehrerkonferenz (en).... staff meeting
der Schulleiter (-)..........head
die Sekretärin (nen)......secretary
die SMV ....school council
der Sprachassistent (en) *wk* .. language assistant
der Studienrat (-räte) ....secondary teacher
die Studienrätin (nen)...secondary teacher

Das Schulgebäude **The school complex**

der Arbeitsraum (-räume) ....private study room
die Aula (Aulen)...........school hall
die Bibliothek (en)........library
das schwarze Brett ....notice board
das Büro (s)..................office
der Fußballplatz (-plätze) ... football pitch
der Gang (Gänge) ....corridor
die Kantine (n).............canteen
das Klassenzimmer (-)...... classroom
das Krankenzimmer (-)..... sick bay
das Labor (s) ....laboratory
das Lehrerzimmer (-) ....staffroom
der Lehrmittelraum (-räume) ....resources centre
der Mehrzweckraum.....multi-purpose room
der Schlafraum (-räume)..... dormitory
der Schulhof (-höfe) .....playground

das Schwimmbad (-bäder) .... swimming pool
das Sekretariat .... school office
die Sporthalle (n).......... sports hall
das Sprachlabor (s) .... language lab
der Tennisplatz (-plätze)..... tennis court
die Turnhalle (n)........... gym
der Umkleideraum (-räume).. changing room
der Werkraum (-räume).... workshop, studio

aus Backstein................ of brick
aus Beton...................... of concrete
gemischt .... mixed, boys and girls

Die Fächer **School subjects**
das Fach (Fächer).......... subject
die Fremdsprache (n).... foreign language
die Kenntnisse *pl*.......... knowledge
das Lernprogramm (e) ...... curriculum
das Lieblingsfach (-fächer) .... favourite subject
die Naturwissenschaft (en).... science
das Pflichtfach (-fächer) .... compulsory subject
das Wahlfach (-fächer) ...... optional subject

Biologie .... biology
Chemie .... chemistry
Deutsch......................... German
Englisch........................ English
Erdkunde .... geography
Französisch.................. French
Geographie .... geography
Geschichte .... history
Informatik..................... ICT
Kunst .... art
Mathe(matik)............... maths, mathematics
Musik .... music
Physik........................... physics
Religion(slehre)............ RE
Spanisch .... Spanish
Sport .... PE
Technologie.................. technology

Berufsberatung .... careers advice
Betriebswirtschaft........ business studies
Drama .... Expressive Arts
Handarbeit .... needlework
Hauswirtschaftslehre ... food technology
Kochen........................ cookery
Latein .... Latin
Medienwissenschaft .... media studies
Sozialkunde .... social science
Turnen .... gymnastics
Werken .... CDT
Wirtschaftslehre........... economics

Der Schultag **The school day**
die Doppelstunde (n) ... double lesson
die Hausaufgaben *pl* .... homework, prep
das Mittagessen (-)....... midday meal
die Mittagspause (n) .... dinner hour
der Morgen (-) .... morning
der Nachmittag (e)....... afternoon
die Pause (n) .... break
der Schulschluss .... end of school day
die Stunde (n) .... lesson
die Versammlung (en). assembly

aufpassen † *sep* .... to be careful, pay attention
die Anwesenheit feststellen *sep* .... to call the register
ruhig sein* *irreg* .... to be quiet
sich setzen †................ to sit down
eine Frage stellen......... to ask a question

For **times** see page 8

Die Schuluniform **School uniform**
die Bluse (n) .... blouse
das Hemd (en)............. shirt
die Hose (n) .... trousers
die Jacke (n)................ blazer
das Kleid (er) .... dress
der Pulli (s) .... pullover
der Pullover (-)............ pullover

der Rock (Röcke) .... skirt
der Schlips (e) .... tie
der Schuh (e) .... shoe
die Socke (n) .... sock
die Strickjacke (n)........ cardigan
die Strumpfhose (n) ..... tights
die Wolljacke (n) .... cardigan

altmodisch .... old-fashioned
praktisch....................... practical
der Reihe nach............. in turn

AGs **Out of school activities**
die AG (s)..................... school club
der Ausflug (-flüge)...... trip, outing
der Austausch (e).......... exchange
der Besuch (e) .... visit
die Blaskapelle (n) .... brass band
der Chor (Chöre) .... choir
der Klub (s) .... club
die Mannschaft (en) ..... team
das Orchester (-) .... orchestra
die Schülerzeitung (en) .... pupil newspaper
das Spiel (e).................. match
die Theatergruppe (en)..... theatre group
das Tournier (e) .... tournament
der Verein (e) .... club

Das Schuljahr **The school year**
die Ferien *pl* .... holiday
die Halbjahresferien ..... February half term
die Herbstferien............ autumn half term
die Osterferien.............. Easter holiday
die Pfingstferien .... summer half term
der Schüleraustausch.... school exchange
das Semester (-)............ semester
die Sommerferien *pl*..... summer holidays
der Stundenplan (-pläne).. timetable
der freie Tag .... day off
das Trimester (-)........... term
der Unterricht .... teaching
die Weihnachtsferien ... Christmas holidays

die Woche (n)...............week
hitzefrei ....day off due to heat

Im Klassenzimmer **In the classroom**
das Fach (Fächer)..........locker, pigeon hole
das Fenster (-) ....window
das Klassenbuch ....class register and record book
die Kreide ....chalk
der Lehrertisch (e) ....teacher's desk
der Schrank (Schränke) .....cupboard
der Stuhl (Stühle) ....chair
die Tafel (n)..................(black/white) board
der Tisch (e).................table
die Tür (en)...................door

der Beamer (-)...............whiteboard projector
der Bildschirm (e).........screen
der Computer (-)...........computer
der Kopfhörer ....headset
das Mikrophon (e) ....microphone
der Schwamm (Schwämme).. sponge
der Tageslichtprojektor (en) ....overhead projector
das elektronische Whiteboard (s) ....electronic whiteboard

die Aufgabe (n).............exercise
der Aufsatz (-sätze) ......essay
der Auszug (-züge) ....extract
der Bericht (e)...............report (of event)
die Grammatik..............grammar
die Hausaufgabe (n) .....homework
die Klassenarbeit (en)...assessment/class test
das Problem (e).............problem
das Projekt (e)...............project
das Symbol (e) ....symbol
der Test (s)....................test
der Text (e) ....text
der Titel (-) ....title
die Übersetzung (en) ....translation
die Übung (en)..............exercise
die Vokabel (n).............vocabulary item

der Wortschatz (-schätze)...... vocabulary list
die Zusammenfassung (en) ... summary

die Aussprache ....pronunciation
das Beispiel (e) ....example
der Fehler (-)................mistake
die Handschrift............handwriting
das Kästchen (-)...........box
die Lektüre ....reading
der Punkt (e)................full stop; point
die Rechtschreibung.....spelling
der Satz (Sätze)............sentence
die Seite (n) ....page
die Sprache (n) ....language
das Wort (Wörter).........(individual) word
die Worte *pl*.................words, statement
die Zeile (n).................line (in text)

die Antwort (en)...........reply, answer
die Aufmerksamkeit.....attention
die Aufsicht.................supervision
der Dialog (e)...............dialogue
die Diskussion (en).......discussion
die Disziplin ....discipline
der Erfolg (e) ....success
das Ergebnis (se)...........result
die Erlaubnis (se) ....permission
der Fortschritt (e)..........progress, improvement
die Leistung (en) ....achievement
die Regel (n)................rule
die Stille ....silence
der Unterricht ....teaching

Die Ausstattung Classroom kit

der Anspitzer ....sharpener
das Bild (er) ....picture
das Blatt Papier............sheet of paper
der Bleistift (e) ....pencil
das Buch (Bücher) ....book
das Etui (s)....................pencil case
der Farbstift (e)............coloured pen
der Filzstift (e).............felt tip pen
der Füller (-) ....(fountain) pen

das Heft (e).................. exercise book
der Kugelschreiber (-).. (ball-point) pen
der Kuli (s).................. (ball-point) pen
das Lineal (e)............... ruler
das Notizbuch (-bücher)....notebook (paper)
der Ordner (-).............. folder, file, binder
der Radiergummi (s).... rubber
die Schere (n).............. pair of scissors
das Schmierheft (e)...... rough book
der Schreibblock (-blöcke) . notepad
das Schreibpapier......... writing paper
das Schulbuch (-bücher) ..... text book
die Schulmappe (n)...... schoolbag
der Stift (e).................. pen
der Taschenrechner (-)........ calculator
das Wörterbuch (-bücher) ... dictionary

der Kleber (-) .... glue stick
der Klebstoff (e).......... glue
die Patrone (n) .... ink cartridge
der Rucksack (-säcke).. rucksack
die Schultasche (n) ...... schoolbag
der Spitzer (-).............. pencil sharpener
die Tinte....................... ink

Nützliche Verben Useful verbs

ankreuzen † *sep* .... to tick (✓)
aufschreiben *irreg sep* . to write down
ausradieren † *sep* .... to rub out, erase
ausschneiden *irreg sep* .....to cut out
beantworten † .... to answer
durchstreichen *irreg sep* ...to cross out
ergänzen †.................... to complete
kleben .... to stick, glue
kopieren †................... to copy
korrigieren † .... to correct, mark
lehren .... to teach
loben .... to praise
ordnen †...................... to put in (right) order
rechnen † .... to calculate
unterstreichen *irreg insep* ..to underline
verbessern † .... to correct
vergleichen *irreg* .... to compare

diskutieren †................to discuss, chat
erklären † ....to explain
fehlen...........................to be absent
notieren † ....to note
studieren †...................to study
verstehen *irreg* ....to understand
sich vorstellen *sep*........to imagine

aufpassen † *sep* ....to be careful; to pay attention
aussprechen *irreg sep*...to pronounce
bedeuten † ....to mean
enden †........................to end, finish
sich entschuldigen †.....to apologise
leisten † ....to achieve
übersetzen † *insep*........to translate
wiederholen *insep* ....to repeat

ausfallen* *irreg sep*......to be cancelled
beaufsichtigen † ....to supervise
erfinden *irreg* ....to invent
erlauben †....................to allow
ermutigen † ....to encourage
Verspätung haben *irreg*.....to be late
herumalbern *sep* ....to play up, mess about

abgeben *irreg sep* ....to hand in
buchstabieren † ....to spell
auswendig lernen..........to learn by heart
Experimente machen....to do experiments
Hausaufgaben machen .....to do homework
nachsitzen *irreg sep* .....to be in detention

plaudern........................to chat
raten *irreg*.....................to guess
schwatzen † ....to chat, gossip

anwesend sein* *irreg*....to be present
eine Frage stellen..........to ask a question
stören ....to disturb
Sport treiben *irreg* ....to play sport
unterrichten *insep* ....to teach
wählen ....to choose

For **daily routine** see page 67
For **modes of transport** see page 59
For **times** see page 8
For **days of the week** see page 8
For **numbers** see page 7

Zukunftspläne **Future Plans**

die Ausbildung ....training course
die Lehre (n) ....apprenticeship
die Universität (en).......university

Arbeit finden *irreg* ....to find a job
arbeiten gehen* *irreg* ...to go out to work
auf die Uni gehen* *irreg* ....to go to university
eine Ausbildung machen ..to train (for job)
eine Lehre machen........to do an apprenticeship
Arbeit suchen................to look for a job

For other **future plans** see page 83

WHAT SCHOOL OR COLLEGE IS LIKE

Wie ist es? **What is it like?**
abwesend .... absent, away
anwesend .... present, here
fleißig .... hard-working
gesprächig..................... talkative
gewissenhaft .... conscientious
Lieblings- .... favourite
Schul- .... to do with school
streng .... strict

dumm .... stupid
durchschnittlich .... average
einfach .... easy
falsch .... wrong
genau .... exact, precise
kompliziert .... complicated
nützlich .... useful
nutzlos .... useless
richtig .... right, true
schrecklich.................... awful
schwierig .... difficult

schwach in .... weak in, not good at
stark in .... good at
nicht gut in.................... not good at

Die Prüfungen **Exams**
die Note (n) .... mark
das Zeugnis (se) .... report

1 sehr gut .... very good
2 gut........................... good
3 befriedigend............ satisfactory
4 ausreichend............. adequate
5 mangelhaft.............. weak
6 ungenügend .... unsatisfactory

das Abitur, das Abi .... A level
das Abschlusszeugnis (se) .. final report
der Abschluss (-schlüsse) ... final qualification
der Hauptschulabschluss .... GCSE
der Realschulabschluss....... GCSE

die Klausur (en) .... A Level module test
der Kurs (e) .... course
die mündliche Prüfung ......speaking test
die schriftliche Prüfung .....written exam
das Zeugnis (se) ....report

For **choice of study** see page 83

die Antwort (en) .... answer
die falsche Antwort ..... wrong answer
die richtige Antwort..... right answer
die Arbeit .... work
das Ergebnis (se) .... result
das Examen (-) .... degree exam
die Frage (n) .... question
die Klassenarbeit (en).. assessment/class test
das Niveau (s) .... level
das Resultat (e)............ result
der Unterricht.............. teaching

Nützliche Verben **Useful verbs**
abschreiben *irreg sep*... to copy
bestehen *irreg* .... to pass (exam)
sitzen bleiben* *irreg*.... to repeat a year
durchfallen* *irreg sep*.. to fail (exam)
Recht haben *irreg* .... to be right
Unrecht haben *irreg*..... to be wrong
mogeln .... to cheat
schwänzen † .... to skive off school
studieren † .... to study
versetzt werden* *irreg*......to move up a class
wiederholen *insep*........ to revise

Das Schulleben **School life**
die Eltern *pl* .... parents
der Jugendliche (n) ‡ ... teenager
der Lehrer (-)............... teacher
die Lehrerin (nen)........ teacher
der Schüler (-)............. school student
die Schülerin (nen) ...... school student
der Teenager (-) .... teenager

die Klassenarbeit (en) .. class assessment test
die Prüfung (en) .... examination
die Schularbeit .... school work
die Schuluniform.......... school uniform

For **school** see page 77

Höhere Bildung **Higher education**
das Diplom (e) .... diploma
die Hochschule (n) .... university
der Hochschulabschluss (-schlüsse)
.... degree
das Staatsexamen (-)..... degree
der Student (en) *wk* ...... university student
die Studentin (nen)....... university student
das Studentenwohnheim (e)
.... hall of residence
der Studienplatz (plätze) .... place at uni
das Studium (Studien) .. (course of) study
die Uni (s) .... university
die Universität (en) ...... university
die Zukunftspläne *pl* .... future plans

Die Studienwahl **Choice of study**
die kaufmännische Ausbildung
.... business studies
die Fremdsprachen .... languages
die Humanistik .... humanities, classics
die Informatik............... ICT
die Jura *pl*..................... law
die Medizin .... medicine
die Musik .... music
die Naturwisenschaften *pl*......science

diskutieren † .... to discuss
erlauben † .... to allow
helfen *irreg* (+ Dat)...... to help
sich interessieren † für ...... to be interested in
sich verbessern † .... to improve
vorziehen *irreg sep* ...... to prefer
weitermachen *sep* .... to continue, carry on
wiederholen *insep* .... to revise

For **school subjects** see page 78

Ein studienfreies Jahr **A gap year**
der Freiwillige ‡ .... volunteer

Man kann ... **You can ...**
Geld verdienen .... earn money
ins Ausland reisen .... travel abroad
viel erleben .... experience lots
die Welt sehen .... see the world
wieder studieren .... pick up your studies
sich das Studieren abgewöhnen
.... get out of the habit of studying

Die Ausbildung **Training**
das Arbeitspraktikum.... work experience
die Ausbildung .... training scheme
der Ausbildungsplatz (-plätze)
.... training place
die Berufsausbildung.... vocational training
das Berufspraktikum..... work experience
das Betriebspraktikum ...... work experience
die Lehre (n) .... apprenticeship
die Volkshochschule (n)... evening classes
die Weiterbildung......... continuing education

ausbilden † *sep* .... to train s.o
sich weiter bilden † ...... to continue education
gute Zeugnisse haben *irreg*
.... to have good reports/references
Diplom machen .... to graduate
Staatsexamen machen .. to graduate
berufstätig sein* *irreg* .. to have a job
studieren † .... to study for a degree

Leute **People**
der Auszubildende (n) ‡ ... trainee, apprentice
der Azubi (s) .... trainee, apprentice
der Bewerber (-) .... applicant
die Bewerberin (nen).... applicant
der Lehrling (e)............. apprentice
der Praktikant (en) *wk*... trainee
die Praktikantin (nen)... trainee

For **professions** see page 86

Druck **Pressure**

der Elterndruck............parental pressure
der Gruppendruck.........peer pressure
der Lehrerdruck ....teacher pressure
der Stress ....pressure of life today

unter Druck stehen *irreg*
................................to be under pressure
Druck setzen † auf........to put pressure on

Schwierigkeiten **Problems**

die Arbeit.....................job, employment
die Bande.....................gang of yobs
der Diebstahl (-stähle)..theft
die Entlassung (en).......redundancy, the sack
der (religiöse) Fanatismus
................................(religious) fanaticism
der Geldmangel ....lack of money
die Markentreue ....brand loyalty
das Mobbing.................bullying
Schulden *pl*..................debt
die Schule....................school
die Schwierigkeit (en)..problem
die Sorgen *pl* ....sadness, trouble

arbeitslos ....out of work
ärgerlich.......................annoyed
begabt ....gifted
benachteiligt ....disadvantaged
erstaunlich ....astonishing
erstaunt ....astonished

gelangweilt .... bored
gespannt....................... tense
gestresst .... stressed out
schlecht informiert....... ill-informed
langweilig .... boring
nervös .... nervous
pflicht........................... compulsory
priviligiert.................... privileged
traurig .... upset
verärgert....................... annoyed
verständnisvoll............ understanding

spät ins Bett gehen*..... to go to bed late
früh ins Bett gehen*..... to go to bed early
spät aufstehen* .... to get up late
früh aufstehen* .... to get up early
Geld verdienen † .... to earn money

schlecht auskommen mit *irreg sep*
.... to get on badly with
betrügen *irreg* .... to deceive
billigen .... to approve of
sich durchschlagen *irreg sep*
.... to get on with it
entlassen *irreg* .... to dismiss, sack
Mitleid haben mit .... to pity
kritisieren †................. to criticise
sich langweilen .... to be bored
verstehen *irreg*............ to understand

CURRENT AND FUTURE JOBS

Samstagsjobs **Saturday jobs**

die Arbeit (en).............work
das Babysitten...............baby sitting
der Job (s)....................job (for student)
der Supermarkt (-märkte)....supermarket
der Teilzeitjob (s).........part-time job

der Arbeitgeber (-)........employer
der Arbeitnehmer (-) ....employee
die Arbeitnehmerin (nen). employee
die Babysitterin (nen)...babysitter
der Kassierer (-)...........till operator
die Kassiererin (nen)....till operator
der Kellner (-)..............waiter
die Kellnerin (nen).......waitress
der Praktikant (en) *wk*..trainee
die Praktikantin (nen)...trainee
der Tellerwäscher (-)....washer-up
der Verkäufer (-) ....sales assistant
die Verkäuferin (nen)...sales assistant

Geld ausgeben *irreg sep*... to spend money
Geld sparen ....to save money
Geld verdienen † ....to earn money

im Monat.....................per month
pro Stunde ....per hour
pro Woche....................per week

arbeiten †.....................to work
im Büro arbeiten † ....to work in an office
bei Lidl arbeiten † ....to work at Lidl
im Supermarkt arbeiten †
......................to work in a supermarket
drinnen arbeiten † ....to work indoors
im Freien arbeiten † .....to work outdoors
austragen *irreg sep*.......to deliver (newspapers)
Feierabend haben *irreg*
...........................to finish the day's work
die Stellenanzeigen lesen *irreg*
...........................to read the job adverts
ein Praktikum machen..to do work experience
Arbeit suchen ....to look for work

Im Betrieb **Business**

die Aufgabe (n).............task
der Beruf (e) ....career, profession
der Betrieb (e)..............business, firm
die Firma (Firmen) ....firm
das Geschäft (e) ....business
der Handel ....trade
die Möglichkeit (en).....opportunity
der Plan (Pläne) ....plan
das Team (s).................team
das Unternehmen (-) .....firm

die Ambition (en).........ambition
die Arbeitsbedingungen *pl*
...............................working conditions
die Aufstiegsmöglichkeiten *pl*
.... opportunites for promotion
die Beförderung (en) ....promotion
die Betriebsferien *pl* .....annual holiday
der Entschluss (-üsse)...decision
die Gehaltserhöhung (en)..... pay increase
die Karriere (n)............(high-flying) career
der Streik (s) ....strike
die Wahl (en)................choice
der Wettbewerb (e).......competition

das Gehalt (Gehälter)....salary
der Lohn (Löhne)..........pay, wages
der Ruhestand..............retirement
die Sozialabgaben.........national insurance
die Steuern *pl*................taxes

im Ausland ....abroad
langfristig ....long term
arbeitslos ....out of work

Informatik-Kenntnisse anwenden *sep*
...............................to use computer skills
Leuten helfen *irreg*.......to help people
eine Uniform tragen *irreg* .. to wear uniform

Leute **People**

The feminine version is not given if formed by adding **-in (nen)** to the masculine noun.

der Angestellte (n) ‡.....employee
der Arbeitgeber (-)........employer
der Arbeitnehmer (-).....employee
der Arbeitslose (n) ‡.....unemployed person
der Auszubildende (n) ‡... apprentice
der (Firmen)Chef (s).....boss
der Direktor (en)..........director, manager
der Geschäftsführer (-) ..... manager
der Kollege (n) *wk*........colleague
die Kollegin (nen) ....colleague
der Lehrling (e)............apprentice
die Leitung ....management
das Personal *sing* ....staff
der Personalleiter (-).....personnel director
der Verkaufsleiter (-)....sales director

pünktlich ankommen* *irreg sep* ....to arrive on time
mit Verspätung ankommen* .... to be late
faxen............................to fax, send a fax
eine E-Mail schicken....to send an email
arbeitslos sein* *irreg*....to be unemployed
gut gekleidet sein*........to be well-dressed
gut organisiert sein* .....to be well-organised

Im Büro **In the office**

Absender/Abs...............Sender
die Akte (n) ....file
die Aktentasche (n) ......briefcase
der Anrufbeantworter (-) ....answering machine
die Besprechung (en)....meeting
der Computer (-)...........PC, computer
das Fax (-)....................fax
das Faxgerät (e) ....fax machine
die Faxnummer (n).......fax number
das Formular (e)............form
das Fotokopierer (-) ......photocopier
die Gewerkschaft (en) ..union
die Mappe (n) ....(thin) case
die Post ....post, mail
das Telefonbuch (-bücher).... phone book
die Telefonnummer (n)......phone number
der Termin (e)...................appointment
der Terminkalender (-).......diary
der Umschlag (-schläge)....envelope

For **ICT** see page 45
For **opinions** see page 10

Berufe **Professions**

der Arzt (Ärzte) .... doctor
die Ärztin (nen) .... doctor
der Beamte (n) ‡ .... civil servant, official
der Berater (-) .... counsellor
der Chirurg (en) *wk*...... surgeon
der Krankenpfleger (-)......male nurse
die Krankenschwester (n)..nurse
der Lehrer (-)................ teacher
der Politiker (-) .... politician
der Polizist (en) *wk* ...... policeman
die Polizistin (nen) ...... policewoman
der Schulleiter (-)......... headteacher
der Sozialarbeiter (-).... social worker
der Tierarzt (-ärzte)...... vet (fem like Ärztin)
der Zahnarzt (-ärzte) .... dentist

der Architekt (en) *wk* ... architect
der Autor (en) *wk*......... writer
der Bibliothekar (e)...... librarian
der Büroangestellte ‡... office worker
der Chef (s) .... boss
der Designer (-)........... designer
der Dolmetscher (-)...... interpreter
der Forscher (-) .... research worker
die Geschäftsfrau (en).. businesswoman
der Geschäftsmann (-männer) .. businessman
der Informatiker (-)...... computer scientist
der Ingenieur (e) .... engineer
der Journalist (en) *wk*... journalist
die Kauffrau (en) .... businesswoman
der Kaufmann .... businessman

die Kaufleute *pl*............ business people
der Meteorologe (n) *wk*.... meteorologist
der Moderator (en) .... TV presenter
der Musiker (-) .... musician
der Naturwissenschaftler (-)...scientist
der Pilot (en) *wk*.......... pilot
der Programmierer (-) .. programmer
der Rechtsanwalt (-anwälte)...lawyer
die Rechtsanwältin (nen) ....lawyer
der Steuerberater (-) ..... accountant
der Techniker (-) .... technician
der Vertreter (-) .... rep(resentative)

der Apotheker (-).......... chemist (dispensing)
der Ausbilder (-).......... instructor
der Bäcker (-) .... baker
der Blumenhändler (-).. florist
der Drogist (en) *wk*....... chemist (non-dispensing)
der Feuerwehrmann (Feuerwehrleute) .... fireman
der Fischhändler (-)...... fishmonger
der Fleischer (-)........... butcher
der Florist (en) *wk*........ florist
der Fotograf (en) *wk*..... photographer
die Friseuse (n)............ hairdresser
der Frisör (e)................ hairdresser
der Gemüsehändler (-)...... greengrocer
der Hotelbesitzer (-)..... hotelier
der Immobilienmakler (-)... estate agent
der Kassierer (-)........... till operator, cashier
der Konditor (en).......... cake specialist
der Ladenbesitzer (-).... shopkeeper
der Metzger (-) .... butcher
der Obsthändler (-)....... fruitseller
der Verkäufer (-) .... sales assistant
der Zeitungshändler (-)...... newsagent

der Bauarbeiter (-)........ construction worker
der Briefträger (-) .... postman
der Elektriker (-)........... electrician
der (LKW-)Fahrer (-) ... (lorry) driver
der Handwerker (-)....... craftsman, tradesman

die Hausfrau (en)..........housewife
der Hausmann (-männer).... househusband
der Kellner (-)...............waiter
der Koch (Köche).........cook
die Köchin (nen)...........cook
der Maurer (-)...............bricklayer
der Mechaniker (-)........mechanic
die Sekretärin (nen)......secretary
der Tischler (-)..............carpenter

der Anstreicher (-)........painter
der Arbeiter (-).............manual worker
der Bauer (n) *wk*...........farmer
der Bauunternehmer (-)...... builder
der Bergmann (Bergleute).. miner
der Fabrikarbeiter (-)....factory worker
der Fischer (-)..............fisherman
der Flugbegleiter (-)......flight attendant
der Fremdenführer (-)...tourist guide
der Gärtner (-)..............gardener
der Hausmeister (-).......caretaker
die Kinderpflegerin(nen).... nursery nurse
der Klempner (-)..........plumber
der Landarbeiter (-).......agricultural worker
der Maler (-) ....painter
der Matrose (n) *wk*........sailor
der Sänger (-)...............singer
der Seemann (-männer) .... seaman, sailor
der Soldat (en) *wk*.........soldier

Der Arbeitsplatz **The workplace**

das Büro (s)...................office
die Fabrik (en).............factory
die Firma (Firmen).......firm
das Geschäft (e) ....shop
das Krankenhaus (-häuser) ... hospital
das Labor (s) ....laboratory
der Laden (Läden) ....shop
die Schule (n) ....school

draußen.........................outdoors
drinnen..........................indoors

LOOKING FOR AND GETTING A JOB

Die Bewerbung **Applying for a job**

das Arbeitsamt (-ämter).... job centre
die Arbeitserfahrung..... experience (of work)
die Ausbildung .... professional training
die Aussicht auf Arbeit .... job prospects
das Bewerbungsgespräch.. job interview
die Bewerbungsunterlagen *pl* .... application papers
der Brief (e) .... letter
die Erfahrung (en) .... experience
der Familienname (n) *wk*... surname
der Familienstand .... family status
das Geburtsdatum .... date of birth
der Geburtsort.............. place of birth
der Kandidat (en) *wk* .... applicant
der Lebenslauf .... CV, curriculum vitæ
der Mädchenname (n) *wk* ...... maiden name
die Mitteilung (en) .... notification
die Qualifikation (en)... qualification
das Staatsexamen (-)..... degree
die Stelle (n)................ job, post
das Stellenangebot (e)... job offer
die Verantwortung........ responsibility
der Vorname (n) *wk*...... first name
das Vorstellungsgespräch (e)... job interview

arbeiten † .... to work
annehmen *irreg sep* ...... to accept
aufgeben *irreg sep*........ to give up
ausgeben *irreg sep*........ to give, hand out
beilegen *sep* .... to enclose
beraten *irreg*................ to advise
besprechen *irreg*........... to discuss
bestätigen †................... to confirm
sich bewerben *irreg*...... to apply
erhalten *irreg*............... to receive
kündigen .... to sack, give notice
liefern .... to deliver
einen Kurs machen....... to go on a course
mitteilen *sep* .... to notify
Rat suchen .... to seek advice

Eigenschaften **Qualities**

die Geduld .... patience
die Gesundheit .... good health
die Höflichkeit .... politeness
die Intelligenz .... intelligence
die Persönlichkeit (en) .... personality, character
der Sinn für Humor...... sense of humour

ehrlich .... honest
erfahren .... experienced
fleißig .... hard-working
geduldig .... patient
höflich .... polite
professionell .... professional
qualifiziert .... qualified
mit Computerkenntnissen... computer literate

die Schichtarbeit .... shift work
die Teilzeitarbeit .... part-time work
die Vollzeitarbeit .... full-time work

fest angestellt .... permanently employed
gut bezahlt .... well-paid
schlecht bezahlt .... badly paid
regelmäßig .... regular, steady
vorübergehend .... temporary

Arbeitszeiten **Working arrangements**

der Ganztagsjob (s)...... full-time job
die Ganztagsstelle (n).. full-time job
die Gelegenheitsarbeit...... casual work
die Gleitzeit .... flexitime
der Nebenjob (s) .... additional job
jobben .... to do casual jobs

pro Stunde.................... per hour
in der Woche .... per week
im Monat .... per month
im Ausland .... abroad
langfristig.................... long term

Teilzeit .... part-time
angestellt .... wage-earning
arbeitslos .... out of work

die Besprechung (en) ... meeting
die Frühstückspause ..... morning break
die Mittagspause (en)... lunch break

Home-Office machen... to work from home

Die Identität **Personal Details**
Frau .... Mrs, Ms
Fräulein .... Miss
Herr (en) *wk* .... Mr
die Adresse (n) .... address
die Anschrift (en) .... address
der Ausweis (e) .... identity card, ID
der Familienname (n) *wk*.... surname
das Foto (s) .... photo
geboren am … .... born on …
das Geburtsdatum .... date of birth
der Geburtsort (e) .... place of birth
das Geschlecht (er) .... sex, gender
die Größe (n) .... height, size
die Hausnummer (n) .... house number
der Nachname (n) *wk* ... surname
der Name (n) *wk* .... name
der Pass (Pässe) .... passport
der Personalausweis (e)..... identity card
die Postleitzahl (en) ..... postcode
der Spitzname (n) *wk*.... nickname
die Staatsangehörigkeit ..... nationality
die Stadt (Städte).......... town
die Straße (n)............... street, road
die Telefonnummer (n) ..... phone number
die Unterschrift (en)..... signature
der Vorname (n) *wk*...... first name
der Wohnort (e)........... place of residence

buchstabieren † .... to spell
pendeln .... to commute
wohnen .... to live (reside)

Am Telefon **Phoning**
am Apparat .... "speaking", (on phone)
Warten Sie auf das Freizeichen! .... Wait for the dialling tone
Bitte, warten Sie! .... Hold the line
das Gespräch (e) .... call, conversation
Einen Augenblick .... Just a minute
Bleiben Sie am Apparat.... Please hold
Ich höre zu .... I'm listening
Ich verbinde Sie .... I'm connecting you
Kann ich etwas ausrichten? .... Can I take a message?
Rufen Sie mich an .... Phone me
Ich rufe Sie zurück .... I'll ring you back
Auf Wiederhören! .... Goodbye

besetzt .... engaged, busy
außer Betrieb .... out of order
falsch verbunden .... wrong number
gebührenfrei .... free call

der Anrufbeantworter (-) .... answering machine
das Faxgerät (e)............ fax machine
das Handy (s) .... mobile phone
der Hörer (-)................. handset
das Kartentelefon (e)..... card phone
das Mobiltelefon (e)...... mobile phone
das Münztelefon (e) ...... payphone
die Telefonkarte (n)...... phonecard
die Telefonzelle (n) ...... phone box

der Anruf (e) .... phone call
der Anrufer (-) .... caller
die Auskunft .... directory enquiries
die E-Mail-Adresse ...... email address
die Faxnummer (n)....... fax number
das Freizeichen .... dialling tone
die Münze (n) .... coin
der Notruf (e)............... emergency call
die Nummer (n) .... number
der Tarif (e) .... rate, charge

das Telefonbuch (-bücher).....directory
die Vorwahl (en) ....code
die Zahl (en) ....figure, number
die Zentrale..................exchange, operator

den Hörer abnehmen *irreg sep*
................................to lift the handset
anrufen *irreg sep* ....to phone (someone)
den Hörer auflegen *sep*......to hang up
faxen.............................to fax
klingeln.........................to ring (phone, bell)
am Telefon sein* *irreg*
................................to be on the phone
sprechen *irreg*..............to speak, talk
telefonieren †................to phone (in general)
verbinden *irreg*............to connect
wählen ....to dial
zuhören *sep*..................to listen
zurückrufen *irreg sep* ...to call back

Am Arbeitsplatz At Work

Vorteile und Nachteile For and Against
die Arbeit am Fließband
...............................assembly line work
die Arbeit im Freien .....outdoor work
die Arbeitszeit ....hours of work
die Arbeit im Sitzen .....a sitting down job
die Büroarbeit...............office work
die Entlassung (en).......sacking, redundancy
die Kündigung (en) ......sacking,
giving notice
die Schichtarbeit...........shift work

gut bezahlt....................well-paid
schlecht bezahlt ....badly paid
gefährlich......................dangerous
langweilig.....................boring

abends arbeiten †..........to work evenings
draußen arbeiten † ....to work outdoors
drinnen arbeiten †.........to work indoors
ganztags arbeiten † ....to work full-time
halbtags arbeiten †........to work part-time

mit dem Computer arbeiten †
.... to use a computer
Tag und Nacht arbeiten †
.... to work day and night
am Wochenende arbeiten †
.... to work weekends

abschließen *irreg sep*... to lock up
aufschließen *irreg sep*.. to unlock
forschen .... to do research
selbständig sein* *irreg*
.... to work for oneself
Uniform tragen *irreg* ... to wear a uniform
reich werden* *irreg* ..... to get rich

Im Ausland arbeiten Working abroad
Man gewöhnt sich an: You get used to:
eine Fremdsprache....... a foreign language
ein anderes Klima........ a change of climate
eine andere Kultur .... a different culture
ausländische Sitten ...... foreign culture

die Einsamkeit .... loneliness
Heimweh .... homesickness

im Ausland arbeiten..... to work abroad
andere Länder besuchen †
.... to visit other countries
Kontakt mit Leuten haben *irreg*
.... to have contact with people
Leuten helfen *irreg*...... to help people
Leute kennenlernen *sep* ....to meet people
reisen .... to travel
Erfahrungen sammeln
.... to broaden one's experience
einsam sein* *irreg* .... to be isolated
isoliert sein* *irreg* .... to be isolated

For **times** see page 8
For **duration of time** see page 9
For **transport** see page 59
For **professions** see page 86

ABBREVIATIONS

ADAC (Allgemeiner Deutscher Automobil-Club) .... car breakdown club
AG (die Arbeitsgemeinschaft) .... (school) club, group
ARD (Arbeitsgemeinschaft der öffentlich-rechtlichen Rundfunksanstalten der Bundesrepublik Deutschland) ... shared TV channel
BH (Büstenhalter) .... bra
BRD (Bundesrepublik Deutschland) .... German Federal Republic
CH (Confoederatio Helvetica) .... Switzerland (in Latin)
cm (Zentimeter) .... centimetre
DB (Deutsche Bahn) .... German railways
DDR (Deutsche Demokratische Republik) .... East Germany (1949-1990)
DIN (Deutsche Industrie Normen) .... standardised industrial specifications
DJH (Deutsches Jugendherbergswerk) .... German Youth Hostel Association
einschl. (einschließlich) .... included
FCKWs (Fluorchlorkohlenwasserstoffe) .... CFCs
Fr. (Frau); **Frl.** (Fräulein) .... Mrs, Ms; Miss
GmbH (Gesellschaft mit beschränkter Haftung) .... Limited Company, PLC
GuK (Gruß und Kuss) .... Love and kisses (in emails, texts)
Hr. (Herr), **Hrn**. (Herrn) .... Mr
inbegr. (inbegriffen) .... included
inkl. (inklusive) .... included
Kfz (Kraftfahrzeug) .... vehicle (with an engine)
Lkw (Lastkraftwagen) .... lorry, LGV (Large Goods Vehicle)
m (Meter) .... metre
MfG (mit freundlichen Grüßen) .... Yours sincerely (in emails, texts)
MwSt (Mehrwertsteuer) .... VAT (Value Added Tax)
Pkw (Personenkraftwagen) .... car
PLZ (Postleitzahl) .... postcode
SMV (Schülermitverwaltung) .... school council, student council
StVO (Straßenverkehrsordnung) .... highway code
USA (United States of America) .... USA
usw. (und so weiter) .... etc (and so on)
z.B. (zum Beispiel) .... eg (for example)
ZDF (Zweites Deutsches Fernsehen) .... German second TV channel
So (Sonntag) .... Sunday
Mo (Montag) .... Monday
Di (Dienstag) .... Tuesday
Mi (Mittwoch) .... Wednesday
Do (Donnerstag) .... Thursday
Fr (Freitag) .... Friday
Sa (Samstag, Sonnabend) .... Saturday

INDEX